I'M STILL HERE

I'M STILL HERE

LOVING MYSELF IN A WORLD NOT MADE FOR ME

AUSTIN CHANNING BROWN

WITH ANDREA WILLIAMS

CONVERGENT BOOKS

NEW YORK

Published in the United States by Convergent Books, an imprint of Random House, a division of Penguin Random House LLC, New York.

CONVERGENT BOOKS is a registered trademark and its C colophon is a trademark of Penguin Random House LLC.

This work is based on *I'm Still Here* by Austin Channing Brown, first published in hardcover by Convergent Books, an imprint of Random House, a division of Penguin Random House LLC, in 2018.

Library of Congress Cataloging-in-Publication Data
Names: Brown, Austin Channing, author.
Title: I'm still here: adapted for young readers / Austin Channing Brown.
Other titles: I'm still here (Young reader's adaptation) | I am still here
Description: First edition. | New York: Convergent, [2023] |
Audience: Ages 8-12 | Audience: Grades 4-6
Identifiers: LCCN 2022036809 (print) | LCCN 2022036810 (ebook) |
ISBN 9780593240182 (hardback) | ISBN 9780593240199 (ebook)
Subjects: LCSH: Brown, Austin Channing—Childhood and youth—
Juvenile literature. | African American girls—Biography—Juvenile literature. |
African Americans—Race identity—Juvenile literature. | African American
Christians—Biography—Juvenile literature. | African American political activists—
Biography—Juvenile literature. | United States—Race relations—Juvenile literature.
Classification: LCC E185.615 .B7335 2023 (print) | LCC E185.615 (ebook) |
DDC 305.896/0730092 [B]—dc23/eng/20220831
LC record available at https://lccn.loc.gov/2022036809
LC ebook record available at https://lccn.loc.gov/2022036810

Printed in Canada on acid-free paper

crownpublishing.com

2 4 6 8 9 7 5 3 1

First Edition

*To all the kids who were the only one or the first one
or the odd one, I'm so glad you're still here*

CONTENTS

Contents

I'M STILL HERE

GROWING UP IN A BLACK GIRL'S BODY

I love being a Black girl. And sometimes being a Black girl in America is hard. This whole book can be summed up in those two sentences. Book report done!

There are many reasons why it can be hard being a Black kid in America. If you are the first generation in your family to be born in America, that can be hard. If English isn't your first language, that can be hard. If you move around a lot and have to change schools often, that can be hard. If you are multiracial, that can be hard. If you were adopted by a family who is a different race from you, that can be hard. If you are growing up in a tough neighborhood, that can be hard. There are so many situations that make being a Black kid complicated.

I grew up in a Black family, but my neighborhood

and my schools were mostly white. As early as preschool, I felt different in my school, like I always stood out. And that made me curious about race. Now, don't laugh, but I'm going to make a confession to you. As a little kid, I thought race boiled down to three basic facts:

1. My hair was different from the hair of all the white girls in my class. When white girls put their hair in a ponytail, it usually swung from side to side, *swish, swish,* left to right and back again. However, when I put my hair in a ponytail, it usually bounced up and down. My ponytails were determined to defy gravity with every step I took! I wasn't sure the difference was important; it just seemed like a difference I could point to.

2. White people love cats. I mean *really* love them. Occasionally, kids would come to school with their arms scratched or with short, red marks streaked across their faces. When we asked, "What happened?" the answer was usually a casual wave followed by "Oh, it was just my cat." It seemed odd that anyone would love a creature that constantly attacked them, but who was I to judge? My assumption only grew deeper when I attended my first sleepover. Kristy Canistra had two cats, and those cats had just birthed kittens. I spent the night surrounded by ten white girls chas-

ing ten kittens, while I hid under a blanket trying to avoid all the claws!

3. I learned to never assume that our food would be the same. If macaroni and cheese was on the lunch menu, I should not expect a three-inch-tall square of baked macaroni noodles held together by a decadent mix of cheeses, egg yolk, and butter. Mac and cheese at school didn't stand up at all. It . . . spread, as if it couldn't wait to touch all the other food on my plate.

My point is, this race stuff was hard to figure out. And if you find yourself confused or exhausted from trying to navigate predominantly white spaces, this book is for you.

I'm going to share stories with you that might help you make sense of yourself and your world. I want to be clear, though. This book isn't a step-by-step guide to make everyone you meet like and accept you. I don't have any cheat codes for you. I wish I did. All I have are my stories of being a Black girl growing up surrounded by mostly white people, and how I still managed to love myself. I hope by reading my story, you are inspired to love who you are and decide for yourself how to take pride in your racial identity. I'll share everything I can think of that helped me make sense of who I am and how I fit into the world.

Our stories won't be exactly the same. But by the time you get to the last word on the last page, I hope you will know you are not alone when things get tricky. And I hope you will be inspired to keep falling in love with who you are.

A NAME

▬

I love being Black. And yet, when I was a kid, white people liked to inform me that my skin color didn't matter. Teachers. Counselors. Coaches. Principals. All were eager to assure me of my own invisibility. It was weird because they also all used the same words to explain it to me. I sometimes wondered if there was some secret video being passed around that told them what to say. If I had to create a playlist for these conversations, these would be the hit songs:

Track 1: "I Don't Even See Color" by the Racially Color-Blind

Track 2: "Character, Not Color" by Misquoting MLK

Track 3: "You Could Be Black, White, Green, or Purple" by Utopian Daydreams

Track 4: "We Are All the Same" by the Well-
  Intentioned

By the time I was eight, I had heard all these "songs"
over and over again. But the common refrains didn't
ring true to me, because in the same school where everyone said race didn't matter, people often looked at
me funny. Teachers looked at me funny. Librarians
looked at me funny. Other kids looked at me funny.
Parents of other kids looked at me funny. If my skin
color didn't matter, why were people always eyeball-
ing me?

For a while, I thought it was because I have a name
that is considered a boy's name. Every first day of school
began the same way. I bounced into class, giddily greet-
ing classmates I hadn't seen all summer. We settled down
when the teacher stood up to begin roll call.

When she got to my name, Austin, I raised my hand
and kept it raised as the teacher scanned the boys in the
class. When none of them moved, we watched the worry
climb her face, concerned that a student was missing on
the first day. She repeated herself: "Austin?"

Hand still raised, I'd tilt my head to the side.

"Yes?" she'd ask.

"Here," I would say.

"Excuse me?" she would respond, looking at me funny.

"Here," I would say. "I'm here." If we had been in a TV show, crickets would've started chirping at this point.

"My name is Austin, and I'm here." I would enunciate every word, giving it time to sink in.

The funny look would linger for a moment longer, then disappear.

"Oh, yes, of course! Thank you, Austin. Emily, are you here?" And she would continue on, letting her moment of utter confusion pass without comment.

By the time I was seven, I'd grown used to white people giving me funny looks. But I was stunned to learn the full reason why.

In my family we went to the library every few days. We checked out so many books at a time, we would find them hiding on the car floor, between the cushions of the couch, or under the mail on the dining table. My mom, little brother, and I all had our own library cards, but we weren't selfish with them. We were always searching for the card with the lowest fines owed. Whichever card would release more treasures into our temporary possession was the winner.

One day we were visiting the library in our neighborhood, the one with an outdoor courtyard in the middle. I stood in line by myself to check out a stack of books. When I reached the front, I slid the librarian my stack and plopped a library card on top.

She scanned my card and frowned at the screen. Most librarians were impressed with the fines we owed; it usually led to a joke about doing our duty to keep the library funded. She did not smile. Instead, she asked, "Is this your card?"

I paused for a second, not entirely sure. I thought I handed her mine, but it was definitely possible that it was my mom's or my brother's. I nodded slowly, but she noticed my hesitation and filled the silence.

"Are you sure?" she repeated. "This card says Austin." And then came the funny look.

Hmm. Another person who thought I would be a boy.

"Yes, that's my library card," I responded, with confidence this time. I waited for her to start stamping my books.

She didn't move. Her furry eyebrows met as she squinted at me. She asked again, this time stretching out the syllables the way adults do when trying to give you a chance to take back a lie: "Are you *suuurrrre* this is *yooouuuurrr* card?"

Now I was annoyed. I resisted the urge to hold up

the line by reading each book in my pile out loud, proving I probably knew my own name. But deep down, I knew she wasn't questioning my literacy. I just didn't fully understand what she *was* questioning.

"My name is Austin," I stated, staring back at her. "That is my library card." This time I didn't move a muscle, daring her to ask me a fourth time.

She didn't. She stamped my books and called, "Next."

I was heated. I marched over to my mother, dropped my stack of books onto a nearby table, and demanded to know why she had named me Austin. (I have always had a slight flair for the dramatic.) My mother let out a soft chuckle but quickly stifled it. She could tell I wasn't kidding; I wanted answers. She began recounting the story of my family lineage and how the last name Austin became my first name.

But I cut her off, "Momma, I know how you came up with my name, but why did you choose it?"

The amusement drained from her face as she walked me over to a set of green armchairs. She started talking in a slow, smooth voice. "Austin, your father and I had a hard time coming up with a name that we both liked. One of us thought to use your grandmother's maiden name, because that would make you the final Austin of that family line."

I already knew this part of the story. I swung my legs

impatiently, the green fabric making the back of my legs itchy.

"As we said it aloud, we loved it," she continued. Then she placed her hand on mine and said, "We knew that anyone who saw it before meeting you would assume you were a white man."

My legs stopped moving.

She kept going. "One day you are going to have to apply for school or for jobs or other things. And your father and I wanted to make sure that you at least made it to the interview."

My brain scrolled through all the times a stranger had said my name in public while looking at someone else. In every instance, the intended target had been not only a boy but a white boy. I didn't quite understand my mother's point about applications and such—an application for the library card still in my hand was probably the only one I had filled out to date. But one thing became clear. People's surprised reaction to my name wasn't just about my gender. It was also about my brown skin. That's why the librarian hadn't believed me. That's why she looked at me so funny. That's why lots of people looked at me funny. None of them knew a name like Austin could be stretched wide enough to cloak a little Black girl.

Turned out, I wasn't the only kid who was regularly

eyeballed. In second grade, the only other Black girl in my class had the name Tiffarah. She had smooth brown skin and wore her hair in the cutest styles. I loved her name and was jealous of her gold nameplate necklace that spelled TIFFARAH in chunky, cursive letters. When her name was called during roll call, teachers looked at her funny, too. Their tongues tripped over her name every single time. I never understood how teachers could easily pronounce European last names even when they contained five syllables and three silent letters, but names like Tiffarah were too difficult. Now I wonder how Tiffarah felt in those moments. Did she get frustrated when people completely mispronounced her name? Did she get tired of constantly reminding people how to say it correctly? Did she ever feel prejudged when she looked into the eyes of our teachers for the first time? Our names were so different, but both of us were regularly being sized up.

I know what it's like to watch someone try to make sense of me—no matter what they say to the contrary. I know what it's like to stand before a teacher and watch their expectations change because my body is not what they expected. I know what it's like to navigate a world where people are surprised we exist in it. But here's the thing. No matter how many times someone has looked at me funny, it hasn't changed the truth. I am a Black girl, and my name is Austin. No one's stink eye has been able to squash me out of existence. A teacher not seeing my hand raised hasn't been able to erase my presence. Looks of confusion haven't been enough to diminish who I am.

In this I was confident. But that didn't keep me from wondering: What exactly are people looking for when they look at us funny?

DISTRUST

━━━━

Throughout elementary school, I was never the only Black person in my class. In earlier grades, I was probably one of three, and every year the number of Black students grew a little larger and a little larger. It was nice to never feel completely alone in a classroom, to look around and see at least a couple of faces that looked like mine. But the truth is, no matter how large or small our numbers were in any given year, the school still felt white.

The only way I knew to describe how a place could feel white was to point out the obvious. The teachers were all white. The administration was all white. The curriculum taught us about white people in history and science and math and social studies (excluding the obligatory two paragraphs on Rosa Parks and Martin Luther King, Jr., of course). The cafeteria food was white. I attended a Christian school, and back then the illustrated Bibles, coloring books, and worksheets featured white people. The books in our school library were by white authors and depicted white characters. It was a lot. (I mean, I like Amelia Bedelia as much as the next person, but I could have used a little diversity.) There was a distinct absence of Blackness.

My home was filled with the writings of Toni Morrison, Langston Hughes, Alice Walker, and Terry McMillan. My school was not. My home was filled with the music of Stevie Wonder, Luther Vandross, and Whitney Houston. My school was not. My home was filled with hair gel, cocoa butter, and satin bonnets. My school was not. Every day I woke up surrounded by Blackness but went to a school where I was expected to represent Blackness.

But there was something else. Something in the air. It wasn't just that I couldn't see myself represented in all these various places within school. There was some other *force* at work.

This force mostly remained invisible—the way you can tell you're in trouble, even when your mom hasn't said anything yet. But there were moments when the fog cleared and what was once invisible was suddenly exposed. I think I was in the fourth grade when it first happened. My classmates and I were lining up to leave for gym class, or perhaps art or music. As I was standing toward the back of the line, Zach, a short white boy in front of me, mumbled something about monkeys and bananas. He wasn't looking at anyone in particular.

"What?" I responded, genuinely confused. I glanced at the bulletin boards around the room, searching for a reason he'd be talking about monkeys.

Zach spun around to stare up into my eyes. Then he spat out the N-word.

Everything stopped. The twelve or so kids in front of him disappeared as my eyes narrowed. My stomach lurched. I had always thought of myself as a good kid, the kid who goes out of her way to be nice to everyone. But in this moment, I had a feeling I was about to surprise myself.

My dad used to tell me a story about his childhood. He said that when he was in junior high, some kid had called him the N-word. My dad kicked him, then watched the kid sail through a plate glass window behind him. My dad never told me what I should do if a white person ever called me that word. I was pretty sure I didn't have permission to kick Zach in his face. But I did know that the anger radiating from my skin was justified.

I leaned toward Zach until I was towering over him. Then I dropped my voice and told him exactly what I thought of him. I knew the teacher couldn't hear me over the noise of the class, and I used that to my advantage. I don't remember exactly what I whispered to Zach, but I do know he never tried me again.

As I replay that moment in my mind, I realize it never once occurred to me to tell the teacher. I didn't think to go to the principal's office, either. I had been attending that school for years. I was well-liked and absolutely would have been believed. But I didn't say anything to anyone with authority because I didn't trust them.

How could I? Were the same teachers who were telling me that my color doesn't matter also going to defend me against this awful language? Were the same people who didn't think it was important that I see myself represented in the classroom going to be as upset as I was? That felt illogical. I didn't believe that anyone in charge would protect me. And because I didn't trust any of the "racially color-blind" adults at my school, I knew I had to figure out how to survive that moment on my own.

And you know what? Zach thought he could get away with it, too. Zach didn't learn this language at school, but he also wasn't afraid to use it. And that's what I couldn't name as a little kid: how a place felt white to me, but also felt white to Zach—white enough that he felt he could safely drop the N-word. What was it, beyond the lack of Black people on our worksheets, that made Zach confident in using a racial slur? That was the invisible force I couldn't describe yet, but knew was present.

I remember being so torn about what to do in that moment. I'm not much of a fighter. But I knew I had to do something. My anger was making my body tremble. All I knew to do was to be mean back, and to do it without calling attention to myself. I was honestly counting on him not telling the teacher, because he'd have to explain what he'd said, too. My gut was right, but my voice was small.

I still can't fully explain why I didn't feel confident in my anger. I was the one who had been wronged, and yet I didn't feel certain that I could make a scene (like I wanted to) in response. Did I just not trust my teachers . . . or did I not trust myself, either? I wanted to believe that one day my voice would be powerful enough to push back against the force, but I just wasn't certain, yet.

SAFETY

Despite its imperfections and occasional bad days, I really liked my school. Yes, it was predominantly white. But it was also mine. I knew everyone, and everyone knew me. I walked the halls with confidence. Sometimes I would sneak into the perfumed staff bathroom instead of using the childish orange stalls I was supposed to. Sometimes I asked for the hall pass, but used it just to wander around. I couldn't change everything about my school. But as a student who was generally well-liked, I knew the power I did have. And I didn't have a problem using it when I needed to.

Mrs. Gilsdorf was my music teacher from preschool through junior high. She was short with a mass of curly black hair framing her face. I had absolutely no skill in her class—I wasn't a great singer, I was terrible at reading music, and I struggled to tell the sounds of instruments apart. Yet her class was one of those rare places where making an effort was more important than achieving perfection.

Mrs. Gilsdorf had an endless supply of energy. In addition to teaching music classes, she planned every music assembly for every grade. From small kids playing recorders to older students putting on whole productions, she guided us through it all. For one performance, she decided to use a pre-made script called *Psalty*. The characters on the cover weren't human—they were songbooks with faces, arms, and legs—but with the addition of blond ponytails, it was clear the authors had made the assumption that white students would be performing the roles. Mrs. Gilsdorf didn't pay those pictures any mind. She often gave the lead to Black kids even though there weren't many of us in the school. She made it clear that she could see us—all of us. She showed up in other ways, too.

One day, two of my friends and I decided to start a singing group. Please allow me to repeat, I was not a great singer, but being in a girl group just sounded *fun*. The idea for the group didn't come out of any specific incident. We weren't running from anything or trying to compete with a similar group created by white students. As the only Black girls in our classroom, we just wanted a space to ourselves. To be honest, even though we were a singing group, the actual singing wasn't all that important to us.

Every couple of days we received a pass to leave our regular class and sing with Mrs. Gilsdorf. For just thirty minutes or so, we belted out do, re, mi, fa, sol, la, ti, do as carefree Black girls. For those few minutes, we were stars on our own stage, dreaming of performances we never actually demanded. We gathered around the piano. Standing behind microphones, we used one hand to point at notes on an imaginary scale while the other hand rested on one ear—as if this would magically help us find our note. We were just cuttin' up. We cheered when we did and laughed hysterically when we didn't. Mrs. Gilsdorf rearranged songs we already knew from our regular music class. We felt a rush of pride hearing the new harmonies fall from our lips. Every now and then, we tried out a new song from Kirk Franklin. We rarely nailed it, but it was a good time trying.

Mrs. Gilsdorf gave us a space I like to call sacred. (*Sacred* is what I call any moment when I can connect deeply with myself and people I love.) In these stolen moments away from class, the force was noticeably absent. Mrs. Gilsdorf didn't expect us to carry ourselves a certain way. She didn't correct our language when we started talking like girlfriends, instead of the way we spoke in the classroom. We were able to high-five and interrupt one another and laugh as loudly as we pleased. We snapped our fingers and moved our hips and booty-bumped one another as encouragement. We were safe with her, safe to be ourselves.

To this day, I don't know how Mrs. Gilsdorf secured permission to do this with us. And I don't know how she squeezed us in. Did she take time out of her lunch break? Or did she work late on those days? I wonder if she had to defend what she was doing with us, or explain why it was only the Black girls from one class. I don't know what was happening behind the scenes. And now I wonder if perhaps that was a gift as well—just being able to show up. If Mrs. Gilsdorf did take risks to create those sessions for us, I'm grateful she believed our time together was worth it. It definitely mattered to me.

SUMMER

When I turned eight, my parents got divorced. I had no idea they were having problems in their marriage; I don't remember them ever fighting or even raising their voices at each other. But when they told my little brother and me that they were separating, it was clear they'd been talking about this for a long time. They already had a whole game plan. My brother and I would stay in Toledo with my dad, and my mother would move two hours away, back to Cleveland, where she was from. We would continue to attend the same school, but on most weekends and during the summer we would be with my mom. It all sounded so reasonable. The reality was much harder.

Because my life had contained very little change until that moment, I wasn't prepared for how quickly I would feel unstable, lonely, and afraid in a new environment. My mom was exceptionally patient with my adjustment. But just as I was getting used to the rhythm of changing homes every weekend, it was summer. Suddenly I wouldn't be just hanging out with my mom on the weekends; I'd be going to summer day camp, where I'd be expected to do unimaginably hard things—like, you know, make new friends.

In Toledo, often surrounded by mostly white people, I felt super Black. I knew things about the world that my white friends and teachers didn't seem to know—like the wonders of cocoa butter and the importance of a silk scarf. We sang white Christian contemporary songs in school, and I always felt a little bad for my classmates because they didn't seem to know that Black gospel versions of these songs existed. I mean, I was so Black, a kid called me the N-word on a regular Tuesday, okay? I was Black, Black.

But when I went to Cleveland for the summer, I was surrounded by Black people. Outside my own family, I had never experienced this before. My Blackness didn't feel so Black anymore. The culture shock was both glorious and intimidating.

I wasn't prepared for the loudness and playfulness when Black kids were free to be themselves. I didn't know about dance competitions and talent shows. I didn't know there were more line dances than just the

Electric Slide. There were no games reciting the books of the Bible here; I had to learn to play spades in this joint.

It was hard to keep up. When the popular song "Weak" by SWV came on the bus radio, all the girls started singing it. I had never heard it before, so I pretended to lip-synch the whole thing. I prayed that the girls around me would continue singing with their eyes closed instead of noticing me.

My cover wasn't blown that day, but it felt like only a matter of time before it would be. I wasn't up on the latest in Black celebrity gossip. I had no idea what friend groups had already been formed, or which schools everyone attended, or how I fit into any of it. I wasn't sure how I had ended up here.

And I was afraid that I would never fit in.

One day I was playing on a jungle gym, around other kids, but not really with them. I didn't know their names and wasn't invited to join the conversation, but I tried anyway. From the top of the oval-shaped structure, a boy stopped playing and looked down at me. "You seem like an Oreo," he said. "Why do you talk so white?"

The air left my lungs. I didn't need the definition of an Oreo. I had never been called one before, but I understood immediately: Black on the outside, white on the inside. For a moment I just stared back at him wishing this moment away. The three or four other kids who were climbing all stopped to look at me. The question hung in the air as I tried to catch the sadness racing through my body before it showed on my face.

I wanted to cry. But not because my feelings were hurt about being called an Oreo. I wanted to cry because I was trying so hard to fit in, and it wasn't working. The other kids knew what I knew: Something was weird about me.

I didn't know the rules, the jokes, the music, the dances, the games. I didn't know how to move through this new environment, and everyone noticed. That's why I was sad. That kid was naming that I was different. I was finally surrounded by all Black kids and all Black counselors, yet had never felt more out of place. Every day felt hard for me. I didn't want it to be hard, but it was.

Looking back up at the kid who'd asked the question, I stammered out a long, convoluted answer: "Well, I'm not from here. I don't live in Cleveland. I'm only here for the summer. My parents are divorced and I'm here visiting my mom. I actually live two hours away with my dad. And my school is a Christian private school, which basically means I'm surrounded by white people a lot . . . and I guess that's why I talk like this?" Even after my long explanation, I ended my statement like a question.

I held my breath, waiting for the laughter or judgment or even a simple follow-up question. But nothing came. All the kids who had stopped to listen just blinked, shrugged, and kept playing.

I finally exhaled, turning around to sit on one of the thin metal bars, hot from the sun. I was so rattled, I barely felt the heat.

I stayed rattled for the rest of the summer. I often sat at a table indoors, in the back of the room where we gathered for lunch every day. I would put my soft purple lunch bag with neon yellow zippers on the table in front of me, wrap my arms around it, and bury my face on top. I tried to tune out all the noise outside and every feeling inside. Whenever a camp counselor came to check on me, I always claimed that I was sick, squinting at them as if the light was hurting my eyes. It wasn't exactly a lie. I did feel sick, just deep down.

It took another summer for me to start finding my way. Even then, there were still some days when I got overwhelmed and retreated to the back of the room. But not every day. I joined in playing kickball. I participated in the dance competitions. (I almost won the Tootsie Roll competition one summer!) I went swimming and watched scary movies. I fell in love with SWV's song "Weak" and learned every word. It was strange to be confident at school but feel so shy in the summer. But that shyness gave me the opportunity to observe—to open my eyes, turn toward the sun, and be able to see that all the kids weren't exactly the same.

Some of them were goofy, and others were more serious, like me. Some were athletic, and others preferred to spend time playing board games and card games. Some were good at dancing and singing, while others broke out in song only because they knew it would make us all laugh at how terrible they sounded.

They did have a lot in common: They were growing up in the same neighborhood, attending the same schools, going to the same churches, listening to the same radio stations and news stations. They went to the same mall and barbershops and grocery stores. Since I didn't live in Cleveland year-round, my connections weren't that deep. But the lack of those connections didn't mean something was wrong with me. And it certainly didn't make me white on the inside. I knew that I was Black through and through. I just had to figure out what that meant for myself.

TIFFANI

T hose first couple of summers in Cleveland were a difficult adjustment. I mostly remained shy and quiet. I existed on the outskirts of every group, not really belonging anywhere, but not being pushed away, either. Every day required my effort to participate until I could retreat to the ease of home.

Then Tiffani came along.

Tiffani lived four houses down from my mom. We were about the same age, but that—and being Black girls—was where the similarities stopped. She was short and spunky, self-confident, and playful. She was loud and cussed and taught me more than a few things about boys. She was everything I was not.

I was tall but quiet, working hard to blend in—or blend away. I was a major bookworm, and my favorite place to read was inside a closet. I wore thick glasses and had pimples all over my face (thanks, puberty). I did not meet the requirements for *cool* on any level.

And yet, Tiffani became my friend.

The first time she invited me over to her house, we sat on the hardwood floor of her living room surrounded by *Ebony* magazines while music blared from her CD player. By the end of the summer, we were going to amusement parks together, practicing gymnastics in the front yard (which mostly meant falling on our heads), and climbing trees in my backyard. We rode our bikes around the neighborhood, danced in the driveway, and played until the streetlights came on. We shimmy-shimmy-cocoa-popped and shimmy shimmy pow-ed every summer. And you know what? I was still pretty awkward.

Even Tiffani couldn't cure me! But her friendship was a gift I won't ever forget. With Tiffani, I was able to be a quirky Black girl while also experiencing her version of Black girlhood. I delighted in the ways she was different from me. I knew her boldness and energy wouldn't magically rub off on me, but it didn't have to. I didn't have to become like her to be seen or accepted or loved. She was fully herself and that allowed me to be myself, too.

These days, I am pretty comfortable with my Black

girlness. But every now and then, I still feel like I'm failing at being a Black girl. I recently told my friend Amena Brown that I sometimes feel she's more Black than me because she went to an HBCU (historically Black college or university). I expected her to nod and say something reassuring, but she surprised me by confessing that sometimes she doesn't feel Black enough, either! Whew. I don't know who came up with this phrase *Black enough,* but I've had enough. Two grown Black women still fighting against an arbitrary standard of Blackness is ridiculous. And yet, the pressure is real.

It's easy for Black folks to feel insecure, even at being ourselves. But here's the thing: we are the standard. We are what it means to be Black. How could we fail? It's not even possible. Our very existence creates the vastness of Blackness, the diversity within our community. Blackness is expansive. It stretches to include us all. Our Blackness is not up for debate or comparison. It just *is.* It is who we are, even if who we are is a little different from our friends and family—like Tiffani and me.

There is enough room in the world for goofy Black girls and quirky Black girls and hood Black girls and loud Black girls and shy Black girls and emo Black girls and artsy Black girls and smart Black girls. There is room for Black skaters and Black fashionistas and Black athletes and Black gamers. The world cannot define our complexities and diversities. There is room for all of us, if only basic (that is, racist) thinking would get out of the way. We can love all the ways we are Black. Because loving all of us is also loving ourselves.

CHURCH

━━━

I grew up accepting Jesus into my heart every Friday afternoon. I attended a Christian elementary school, and every week we had a chapel service. These services usually consisted of singing (white) contemporary Christian songs, reading a passage from our (white) illustrated Bibles, listening to a (white) speaker share a testimony or a sermon, and finally accepting (white) Jesus as our savior. (All the artwork around school literally depicted a blond-haired, blue-eyed white Jesus.)

Our chapel services mostly revolved around how to be nice. We heard sermons on being kind to one another, never telling lies, the importance of not cheating, and how we should look out for our siblings instead of fighting with them. Every service was simple, quiet, and serene. After the songs and readings and teachings, I dutifully accepted Jesus into my heart. When you're a kid, you feel like you have to be sure of some things, especially where you will be spending eternity. The best you could hope for during a chapel service was that the speaker for the day would at least be funny. Otherwise, the emotion you were most likely to experience was guilt.

This was the only version of Christianity I knew. I had occasionally attended church with my grandparents—a traditional conservative Black church—but I was usually too busy looking at all the church hats to notice much else. So, when I walked into a youthful Black church at ten years old, I was blown away by the differences between this place and every other worship service I'd encountered.

On that first Sunday, as we wandered down a fluorescent-lit hallway toward the sanctuary, the air was filled with the smell of perfume. Along the way members of the congregation welcomed us, the women in bright dresses and dark stockings, the men in suits, ties, and snakeskin shoes. Everyone we passed greeted us with a warm "Good morning!" as if they already knew us.

We waited a second at the wooden doors outside the sanctuary because the people inside were in the middle of prayer. But soon an "Amen" in unison filled the air, and the double doors swung open. Sunlight poured in from the stained-glass windows lining the far wall. Pea-green carpet stretched the length of the sanctuary. The electric organ had started playing, and everyone was standing on their feet, swaying back and forth. Hands clapped to the beat of the song.

I looked up into the choir stand, filled with brown faces like mine. The choir director moved her hands up and down, in and out. Every member paid close attention to what she was doing. I later learned this was because the choir rarely sang any song the same way twice. She wasn't just conducting prewritten music; she created a new song for us every Sunday. We rewarded her with shouts of "Sing, choir!" and our own melody of hallelujahs.

What may appear as chaotic to an outsider felt like a gentle current to me, carrying me from the beginning of the service to the end. I loved how the church mothers dug into their purses to pull out hard peppermint or butterscotch candies in case we got hungry. I loved the deep resonance of the deacons as they stood shoulder to shoulder singing about all that God had done in their lives. I knew exactly when Sister Johnson was going to catch the Holy Ghost, and I memorized the ushers' hand signals to tell one another that Sister Johnson needed a lap cloth again.

Sunday after Sunday, what grabbed my attention more than anything was the pastor. In the sermons he preached, Jesus sounded like a Black person dealing with the familiar hardships of life—injustice, discrimination, the pain of being called derogatory names. Pastor would read a passage of Scripture filled with *thee*s and *thou*s. Then he would take the time to restate what happened in present-day language we could all understand. The disciples didn't just walk somewhere, they "rolled deep." Bible characters suddenly sounded as real as all of us. Any given Sunday, the heart of the message was the same: *God is with us.* I fell in love with a Jesus who saw our humanity, a Jesus who loved and reveled in our Blackness.

I was an adult before I read any Black theologians or studied Black liberation theology—but when I did, it all felt so familiar. I had already met this Jesus at ten years old, in a Baptist church where the Spirit moved us every week. There Jesus cared about my soul, but he also cared about what it was like to move through the world as a Black girl who often felt unseen and misunderstood. Every Sunday I was reminded that troubles don't last always, that heartbreak and struggle weren't the end of my story.

There was still much to learn: speaking in tongues, prophetic announcements, revival services, and being instructed to talk to your neighbor. (Not to mention, I hadn't realized you could be in such a large group and everyone could clap in time on the two and four. Like, everyone!)

Our church was filled with plenty of drama for ya mama, don't get me wrong. It wasn't perfect. But I felt at home in this place where Blackness was core to its very existence, its movement, its purpose. It was inspiring. It showed me that my school didn't have the last say on spirituality.

Blackness could turn everything on its head.

PUSHING BACK

Being in Cleveland and discovering a newfound joy in a Black church made me a little impatient with the shenanigans of white people. My first subversive act was monumentally . . . small. Like teeny-tiny, itty-bitty, no-one-even-noticed small.

When I was in fifth grade, many of the white girls had long hair. It wasn't unusual for them to accidentally sit on it and yelp in surprise—it was that long. And believe me, you would find their hair everywhere. It was in the bathroom sinks. It was hanging from the water fountain. It was left behind on the desks. I usually dismissed this as a minor annoyance and simply switched sinks, fountains, or seats respectively. But the thing that really bothered me was when a student sat in front of me and their hair spread across my desk.

I was tired of feeling like I was expected to let others

take over what little space I had to claim in the classroom. Back then, I didn't ask for much. I didn't demand a diverse curriculum. I didn't demand more people of color be hired on staff. I didn't demand that teachers stop using references I didn't understand. All I wanted was for my desk to be mine. And one day I'd had it.

A girl with long blond hair sat down in front of me. Her ponytail cascaded over the back of her seat and onto my desk. For a moment, I glared at it. Today it was going to be me or it. I grabbed my yellow number-two pencil, flipped it around in my hand, and used the eraser end to push the ends of the girl's hair off my desk. I smiled as it hung limply in the crack between our seats. I leaned back with great satisfaction admiring my handiwork. She didn't notice at all.

That's it. That was the whole rebellion. That was my first act of claiming my own space. Even though it was small, I'm still proud of it.

At this point I hadn't quite made sense of my annoyance and anger. I could feel it rise and fall, but I couldn't describe how it shape-shifted in my body. If I couldn't describe it, was it safe to express it? I honestly didn't know. Turns out my mother would unknowingly show me one way of expressing it.

My family was gathered in my grandmother's house for a holiday. We all sat around two tables—one for the adults and one for the kids—separated by a short open bookshelf filled with vintage bells my grandmother had been collecting for decades. From my folding chair at the kids' table, I peered through the gaps in the open shelves, trying to follow the adults' conversation as my mom went toe-to-toe in a debate with the men sitting across from her.

"I'm just not sure integration has actually helped Black Americans," she said. Her hands danced in front of her as she continued the impassioned monologue, her afro nodding in agreement.

"Well, what was the alternative, Karen?" one of my uncles retorted. "Remaining in segregation?"

Her eyes flashed. She knew she had them. "Of course not. I'm just saying that *segregation* didn't have to be followed by *integration*. Surely regulating us to the back of the bus could have stopped without us having to give up all the Black businesses that died because of integration. I mean, could we have kept a greater number of Black educators if we had demanded equal funding for our schools rather than busing ourselves to theirs?"

The debate continued, their deep voices rising and falling. Conversations like this were common in our family, but they usually left me bored. For the first time I was intrigued. My mom was questioning history. My school was not teaching me how to do that! If she could, maybe I could, too. And that's how I discovered the art of pushing back. I never raised my voice at an authority figure or shouted at a teacher. I realized that I could be quiet and still resist easy, traditional answers. When I was supposed to say that Christopher Columbus discovered America, I would write that he ravaged and stole it. When I was supposed to praise Abraham Lincoln for the Emancipation Proclamation, I added a line about Frederick Douglass. The first time I had to write a book report, I chose Harriet Tubman as my subject. Anytime I had a reading list, I found the Black authors on it—or I put some Black authors on it, you know what I'm saying? Pushing back on the answers I was supposed to give worked for me. That was the way I felt empowered to speak up, even when it cost me. I was a straight-A student and was well aware that my antics could impact my grades. I did it anyway. It was always worth it.

I was still a little mad at myself for not being a gum-snapping, neck-rolling, don't-think-I-won't-make-a-scene-up-in-here Black girl, though. I desperately wanted to be her. (God bless you if you are that Black girl, because girls like me needed to see your bravery.) But for a while, quietly countering the curriculum worked for me. It served as a helpful outlet for me to be honest. Plus, I knew my parents had my back. Even if my grades suffered, the same man who kicked someone through a window for using the N-word was not about to have me in the principal's office for telling the truth about Christopher Columbus, right?

Pushing back felt like an exercise in getting my facts straight, quietly correcting narratives and daring my teachers to tell my parents. I don't know if they ever did. I suspect many of them liked me well enough to consider me precocious (a fancy word for quirky) rather than disrespectful. And for the most part I really liked school. I enjoyed learning. I loved writing and all the creative classes, like music and art. Gym class was not my jam, but that's mostly because I kept forgetting to put on a training bra—very embarrassing when you're changing in the locker room.

Soon it was time to leave my beloved school behind. I had been there from preschool through the eighth grade. There were never more than thirty kids in any of my classes. But at Central Catholic High School, my freshman class alone contained four hundred students. It was another major transition, but this time I was ready . . . or so I thought.

THE MASK

—

Mr. Slivinski was the first teacher I wanted to put in my pocket and carry around with me all day every day. He was my freshman English teacher and the first to expose me to an intentionally diverse curriculum. Mr. Sli was small but mighty. We weren't sure if his abundance of energy was natural or from drinking coffee out of the warm pot he kept in his classroom at all times. On the first day of school, he informed us that his goal for the year was to give us a headache from thinking so hard. And he often succeeded. There were passionate discussions of Richard Connell's story "The Most Dangerous Game," line-by-line readings of Shakespeare, and assignments to analyze the character development in Daphne du Maurier's *Rebecca*. Through all of this, Mr. Slivinski inspired us to think hard about the assumptions we held about culture, ethics, and laws. He wanted us to color outside the lines of our black-and-white thinking.

Mr. Slivinski's lesson plans would follow our textbook for a few weeks, and then break away for the sake of adding some diversity. One of those breakaways was a unit on poetry. Each day, Mr. Slivinski would hand us printed copies of poems that weren't in our textbook. Each time, he instructed us to read them and mark up the page. Which words stood out? What did we notice about the structure? How did the content make us feel?

One day, Mr. Sli passed out a poem entitled "We Wear the Mask." I started reading immediately. The author's name, Paul Laurence Dunbar, was familiar to me. My stepmom was a high school English teacher, and she often quoted passages of poetry, delighting us as our kitchen became her stage. So when the poem landed in front of me, I knew we'd be reading about the Black experience. Still, my eyes widened when I read the words:

Why should the world be over-wise,
In counting all our tears and sighs?
Nay, let them only see us, while
We wear the mask.

A mask. My mind raced, wondering how often I did this without much thought. Were there parts of me that I kept buried from white people—even the ones I counted as friends? Things did feel different when I was the only Black girl in the class, versus when I was surrounded by Blackness at the lunch table. Was I wearing a mask when I silently challenged my teachers? Was there some sort of comfort I was seeking by not letting them be "over-wise" about how I felt when they chose "racial color blindness" instead of embracing diversity? When I finished the poem, I felt both relieved and saddened. I looked up at Mr. Slivinski in the still quiet room, wondering, *How do you know?*

When I realized he was about to open up the floor to discussion, I folded myself into my chair, trying to make my body smaller, trying to disappear. *Will you make me explain this? Will you ask me to tell an all-white classroom about the masks Black people wear?*

I was surprised by my own reaction. It was deeply gratifying to have my own experience named, lifted up, discussed, considered worthy of everyone's attention. And yet, I had no desire to be the Black spokesperson. It felt too risky. I wasn't sure I was prepared to give my classmates access to such a tender place in my story. For me, this was more than an educational exercise. This was how we survived.

I also wasn't sure I had the right to share. I mean, I could have talked about my own personal experience, but did I have a right to speak on behalf of all Black people? It's not like we had a committee meeting every Wednesday night to decide what we thought about any given issue. How could I possibly convey the reasons and the importance of our mask—from Paul Dunbar's time to today? I was making the connections myself in real time. There was no way I could offer my classroom the weight this topic deserved.

Fortunately, Mr. Slivinski didn't call on me to respond to the poem. Though we had not exchanged a single word since the exercise began, I sensed that he respected my decision not to raise my hand. It was clear to him that I wanted to keep my thoughts private. I listened as my classmates engaged with the content of the poem, trying to imagine what Dunbar was trying to communicate . . . and why. No matter how reasoned their responses, they just couldn't *know*. But that didn't stop Mr. Sli from challenging them. It was the first time I realized that discussing race in the classroom didn't have to be terrible!

I was so grateful that Mr. Slivinski was equipped to navigate that conversation without making me the momentary substitute teacher. He already had my respect, but that day, he also gained my trust. I just wished he could have steered these discussions in every classroom.

THE CONFESSION

———

Sister Phillips was another favorite teacher in high school. She was short with a square frame and a foul mouth, which was intriguing since she was a nun teaching our religion class. She mostly donned mom jeans and oversize plaid shirts. She had a big laugh and told big stories. As she taught from behind her podium, her energy filled the room. Sister Phillips gave us life lessons right alongside the curriculum (and sometimes *instead* of the curriculum). She told us about living in community with other women, sharing resources, and prioritizing friendships and intimacy. There was a bond between Sister Phillips and us, and her classroom crackled with life.

One day after Sister Phillips told us about her fear of ghosts, we stole the remote to the classroom TV and spent the class period secretly turning it on and off. At first Sister Phillips was skeptical, convinced we had figured out a way to control the television. But as the class wore on and the TV continued turning on and off, she started testing it. "If you are my uncle, turn off now," she countered. Off went the TV. She turned to us, eyes wide, and kept testing it by calling out the names of dead relatives. Minutes later, when we burst into laughter and revealed the truth, she wasn't mad at all. In fact, she dubbed us the best class she'd ever had.

Another day, it was Sister Phillips who caught us off guard. As we filed into her classroom, she announced she would no longer use a seating chart. For the first time, we scanned the room and saw nothing but opportunity. We could sit wherever we wanted.

Once we were settled, Sister Phillips informed us that she wanted to share why we had suddenly been given permission to choose our seats. There was something uncharacteristically soft about the way she spoke, and we all leaned in, eager to hear. "Every year I use a seating chart," she began, "deciding where each of you will sit. Earlier this week I realized that my use of a seating chart is racist."

I froze. I was one of only three students of color in the room. I had no idea what was coming next, but I instantly became incredibly aware of my body.

"You see," she continued, "I have been using a seating chart to separate Black students. I didn't fully realize it until I failed to separate two Black young women in one of my classes. When I saw them together, I panicked, thinking, *Great, now they are going to laugh and talk through the entire period.*"

She paused, swallowing back tears. She was clearly overwhelmed, yet making an effort to be as forthcoming as she would be about anything else. She did not mince words or sugarcoat any part of her thinking.

"That's when I realized what I was doing was racist. I have never, ever wondered if any of my white students were going to be disruptive. I've never been nervous to find two white girls sitting next to one another. I am so disappointed with myself, and from now on, you all will sit where you want to sit."

She took a deep breath, and so did I. I'm guessing there were plenty of classes in which Sister Phillips had had to separate two white students for being disruptive. However, by her own admission, this tendency toward disruption was never attributed to their race. Only when the disruptive students were Black did race become a defining factor.

I sat with her words for a minute and tried to make sense of my competing thoughts. While I was grateful that Sister Phillips had had an epiphany—or at least *wanted* to be grateful—her revelation made me self-conscious. I thought so much of Sister Phillips; I wasn't prepared to hear what she had thought of me, of my body. The stereotype about sassy, disrespectful Black girls was not lost on me, but until then, I had thought it was just a convenient, albeit boring, movie trope. I didn't realize it could be used against me.

I looked around the classroom to gauge the response of the other students. No one had anything to add; I think most of them were just glad to be able to sit wherever they wanted. But I was having an entirely different experience. Should I have been happy about my teacher's aha moment? Were there other ways I'd been unknowingly harmed, back before she was aware of her bias? And what about the other teachers at my school, including the ones I liked? Were they also watching and judging me?

In a strange way, it felt like I finally had an answer to the question I had been asking for most of my life. *Why were people looking at me funny?* Because they were always assessing and reassessing their expectations of me. They expected a white boy and got a Black girl instead. And this wasn't just happening to me. Other Black kids and students of color were being assessed, too, sometimes before we even got into the classroom. We were all being measured against a set of unspoken expectations with no idea how we were being graded.

Sister Phillips had always seemed to like me. Did she view me as "the exception," like I was somehow different from all my Black girlfriends? Or had I not been stealthy enough when whispering in class, and only reinforced her stereotypes? I would never know because I never asked—I suspected neither answer would bring me any comfort.

To tell the whole honest-to-goodness truth, I was also a little intrigued by her confession. It's not every day you hear someone in a position of authority admit to doing something racist and make a commitment to stop. Did I want more of this or less of this? Could I be mad at Sister Phillips and proud of her at the same time? Was I allowed to still like her? I had so many questions for myself. Even now, I feel a mix of emotions about that day. I kind of wanted one simple, clear emotion. Mad. Happy. Sad. Instead, there I was, feeling a mix of all of them. I still do. Turns out that's pretty normal when navigating race in America as a Black person or a person of color. Feeling a lot of different emotions at once is another way in which we embrace our own humanity— and make sense of the people in our lives who make mistakes and awkwardly try to fix them.

CHOIR

———

Of course, navigating complicated racial realities wasn't my entire high school experience. I had a blast, too. Plenty of football games, pep rallies, school traditions, and teen drama kept me occupied in between tests.

One of the places I loved most was our Gospel Choir. On Mondays, Wednesdays, and Fridays, Black students from every class piled into our respective sections to socialize—I mean sing! Our choir director was Brother Hammond, an energetic Black man whose passion for music and remixes very much reminded me of Kirk Franklin. Extraordinarily generous, he cared for each of us as if we were his own.

I know this is going to sound silly, but Gospel Choir was the place to be. We didn't just have practice, we had fun. We often got into trouble for how much fun we were having, but Bro Hamm (as we called him) exercised a ton of patience. We loved singing so much that members often stayed late, gathered around the piano to sing anything that came to mind. I remember one afternoon when Gospel Choir was over, someone broke out singing, "Joyful, joyful Lord we adore thee," like Lauryn Hill in *Sister Act 2*. We all chimed in, singing every part along with the coordinated dance moves. We sang as if we were performing to win our own trophy! We giggled through the whole thing, surprising ourselves with how well we remembered every line and every motion.

Across the hall from our practice room was Glee Club. And the two choirs couldn't have been more different. Gospel Choir contained all Black students, while Glee Club contained all white students. Gospel Choir was only half a credit. Glee Club was a full credit. Gospel Choir had little to no budget and was always threatened with being cut. Glee Club had a healthy budget and numerous donors. Gospel Choir performed for free at different churches around the city. Glee Club had ticketed performances in a beautiful theater. I'm not sure members of the Glee Club knew about all these differences, but all the Gospel Choir students did. We didn't make much of a fuss about any of it, until the school administration came for Bro Hamm.

It was the end of a school year, and the administration announced that it might not have room in the budget for Bro Hamm to continue as our choir director . . . or if he did, there might be a severe pay cut. We already knew he wasn't being paid well because our course was only half a credit. And he certainly wasn't being compensated for the ways he went above and beyond his job requirements. He often drove us to and from concerts, fed us when practice ran long, hosted gatherings in his home—and don't get me started on how many hours he spent counseling us through problems at home or at school. We were livid that the administration didn't value him as much as we thought they should. So, we made a fuss.

We started openly discussing the discrepancies in how we were treated compared to Glee Club. Much to our surprise, as soon as the Glee Club members started hearing about the differences, they joined the cause!

They started advocating for our choir director. They asked questions about the budget. (I'm not sure the school made too many changes on this front, but it still mattered that students who benefited from an outsized budget were questioning it.) They made sure that during school assemblies, the Gospel Choir had the chance to perform as often as they did. The two choirs even performed together for one school assembly, and it was amazing.

By the next year, the Glee Club had many Black members. Glee Club students hadn't realized that Gospel Choir members were just as obsessed with musicals as they were! It was amazing to sit in that gorgeous theater and cheer for our friends as they shimmied, box-stepped, and kick-ball-changed across the stage. We had bouquets of roses ready for them and all our friends in Glee Club.

I don't remember any Glee Club members joining Gospel Choir, but I do remember both choirs feeling more connected to each another—playing around in the hallway, showing up at each other's practices, offering our support to one another. Gospel Choir was still the place to be, but it was no longer the *only* place we could be.

AFFIRMATION

━━

Truth be told, Black students found all kinds of ways to connect with one another. We all had white friends, but there was something particular about being together—just us. We formed our own groups in the hallways, sat together in classrooms without seating charts, and, of course, always found each other at lunch time.

But for whatever reasons, other folks felt the need to comment on our tendency to seek one another out. "Why do all the Black kids sit together?" is a question I've heard many times. I heard it in elementary school. I heard it in middle school. I heard it in high school. I heard it in college.

Why do all the Black kids sit together? The question was usually loaded with insinuations from white students and even teachers, as if our desire to sit together was wrong or offensive.

Being together was good for us—even though it made us highly visible.

Our lunch table was always getting into trouble for being "too loud." Black students were regularly asked to disperse as we stood in front of our lockers. Other students complained that they felt unsafe when we were all gathered together, apparently taking up too much space. Meanwhile, I watched as white students routinely ignored policies. They pulled pranks, started food fights, acted out, were loud, and didn't fret over breaking the rules. All of this was usually dismissed as "kids being kids." Their behavior was normalized. But our behavior was scrutinized.

This was especially true regarding our school's dress code. Our uniforms consisted of one shirt (a white button-down), a sweater or vest option, two skirt options, and two pants options. If you could afford all those pieces, of course. But adhering to the dress code wasn't just about wearing the right items of clothing—we also had to wear them the right way. Those button-down shirts couldn't be too tight, and we could unbutton only the top two buttons. Those skirts had to be a certain length—no creating a miniskirt out of your uniform skirt by rolling the waistband. The pants couldn't be altered, either.

You probably can guess where this is going. Black girls' bodies were assessed extra closely when it came to our uniform. Were we wearing it correctly? Did our bodies appear inappropriate in some way? If our curves changed the fit of the shirt or the length of the skirt, was that seen as immodest and therefore disrespectful?

While sitting in religion class one day, our teacher, a priest, stopped his lesson because a student had walked in late. She was tall with thick blond hair, an unusually deep voice, and pale blue eyes. At first, the teacher simply greeted her, but then he realized her skirt was *waaay* above the minimum length. Father Robbie asked her if she realized that her skirt was not meeting the uniform code. She smiled and innocently asked, "What do you mean?" Undeterred, he repeated his statement about her skirt. The girl laughed, knowing he was absolutely right, but she continued to feign ignorance. Now it was a game of wits.

Father Robbie asked her to stand back up to prove his point. She did. She also continued to giggle, even as she argued. They went back and forth until she finally conceded, at which point they both had a good laugh. The girl sat back down, and we continued on with the lesson. She didn't get sent to the principal's office. Even though she'd argued with the teacher, her actions weren't considered disrespectful. The exchange was considered cute.

As this was happening, I turned around to look at Ashlee and Brande, the other two Black girls in the classroom. We shook our heads. We knew we could never get away with that. I wrote on a small piece of paper, "Y'all seeing this?" and discreetly set it on Ashlee's desk. Brande leaned over to read it, and quickly wrote, "GIRL" in all capital letters. We tilted our heads at one another, giving the Black girl facial expression for "You ain't telling no lies." We all knew that if we had ignored the rules like this, we would have landed in the principal's office, detention, or *something*. It was an unfortunate truth that we'd come to accept because we knew we couldn't change it. But we also knew it was unfair. We didn't deserve to be treated differently.

That Black girl affirmation was vital. I didn't realize I was only beginning to scratch the surface of how important our secret language was. We didn't just need one another at the lunch tables to talk about music and movies. We were starved for a certain connection, a certain knowing. We were honing our "Black girl spidey sense." We have inducted one another into a community that can speak in code, via our lingo, sounds, facial expressions, and sometimes just a look. We know how to say what needs to be said, without giving our thoughts away. We wear the mask. In a situation that could have felt isolating, we were bonding. In a situation that could have made us upset, we were trying not to giggle at one another's expressions. In a situation that could have been hard, we were affirming our own existence. The world can make it hard, but I love being a Black girl.

RECEIPTS

—

My parents were intentional about teaching me that it wasn't just teachers who might treat me differently. They wanted me to understand that being Black in America could open me up to scrutiny at any time. This initiation is commonly called "The Talk." It describes the conversation parents have with their kids about how to stay safe in a world that sometimes assumes the worst about us. But for me, there wasn't just one conversation about being a Black person in public; there were several.

Once I was following my dad through the toy section of a local party store when I picked up a little trinket that caught my attention. "Don't even think about it," he said, shutting me down before I could debate whether to ask him to buy it. I sighed, put the trinket back, and stuffed my hands into the pockets of my overalls, willing myself not to be tempted again.

My father glanced back at me. When he noticed my fists bulging from my pockets, he stopped in the middle of the aisle and turned all the way around. "Don't do that," he said sternly.

Do what? I wondered to myself. I hadn't said a word. I'd long ago learned to tame my smart mouth with my dad. Was he now reading my mind?

"Don't ever do that," he repeated more softly this time. He bent his six-foot-two frame toward me to let me know I wasn't in trouble. He gently removed my hands from their denim hiding place. But I was still confused. What had I done wrong?

"Even if you put it back on the shelf, Austin, you can't touch store products and then put your hands in your pockets," he explained. "Someone might notice and assume you are trying to steal."

I nodded. It took some time, but eventually I trained myself not to touch my pockets—or backpack or purse—when walking through store aisles.

Then there was the moment when my mom took me to the mall to buy my first CD. I spent far longer than I should have combing through the thin boxes, deciding between new releases from Boyz II Men, Aaliyah, Mariah

Carey, and Tevin Campbell. I chose Mariah Carey's *Music Box,* took it to the front of the line, and paid for it with the little cash I had. On our way out of the store, I tore into the plastic and opened the CD liner, where artists kept photos and lyrics.

"Whoa, daughter," my mother warned.

I looked at her, utterly confused, wondering if I had shown too much excitement. Even the cashier paused for a moment, surprised by my mother's sudden forcefulness.

"You never open an item in the store," my mother said. "And always have the receipt in your hand if you do. You always want to be able to show someone you paid for your things."

These are examples of the ways my parents prepared me for being a Black girl in America. They created small but impactful moments, teaching me how to protect myself from the assumptions and suspicions of other people.

The lessons were ongoing:

- If you're ever lost, stay where you are and wait for a Black woman to come by, especially if she's a mom. Tell her you're lost and need help.
- If you get pulled over by the police, keep your hands still and ask for permission before you

make any movement, even when obeying their
instructions.
- If you're walking into a store, be sure to remove
your hood or hat so that your face isn't covered.

The lessons weren't difficult to learn, but they were—
and are—disheartening. It's brutal learning that people
will treat you differently just because of your skin
color—not because you *did* something suspicious but
because they have convinced themselves that you *are*
suspicious.

It's possible to grow accustomed to these things, especially when you're with other Black people who are
following the same rules. And once you've been accused
of stealing, or been followed through the store, or been
pulled over, you suddenly understand the importance of
the lessons.

But things get awkward when you're out with friends,
and you're the only Black person in the group. It's weird
watching in real time how different our experiences are,
how others don't have to live by the same rules we were
taught. When our friends are free to do as they please,
but we are on high alert, things can get tricky.

Here's an extreme example. When I got to college,
I discovered there was a tradition called the Freshman

Streak. Every year the freshman boys would choose a day (keeping it secret from the administration), and around midnight run through campus completely naked. Yes, you read that correctly. I'm guessing I don't have to tell you that this concept was completely foreign to the Black freshman boys (and girls, for that matter). We didn't live in a world in which we could get away with such mischief or (*cough, cough*) crime. In fact, most of the lessons we learned about being in public were about making ourselves as inconspicuous as possible. Public nudity is very conspicuous.

I imagine it was a strange moment for any Black freshman who had to explain why he was staying behind. When we are in predominately white situations, we don't have paper receipts proving why our hesitation (or our refusal) to participate is wise. All we have are our stories—and those around us choose whether to believe our account of what America is like for us.

I have found that my closest friends never need receipts. They never need me to repeat a terrible encounter or retell a traumatic story before being believed. All I've ever had to say is, "This makes me uncomfortable." In fact, the friends I trust the most will speak up on my behalf, so I don't have to be the first (or only person) to voice discomfort.

I don't understand why white people often feel the need to leave the city for leadership development retreats, but one such training required our group to travel along some dirt roads. We stayed in a cabin together, so I was cool until someone suggested we leave our secluded abode. We were going to have dinner at the nearest diner where I would definitely stand out. It was already awkward being the only Black person in our group. Now I would be the only Black person in a diner full of strangers in the middle of nowhere? That sounded stressful. Before I could even voice my concern, a friend spoke up, "Listen, we passed by a lot of Confederate flags on our way here, and it doesn't seem fair that Austin would have to eat while being on high alert at this diner. We've got a kitchen. Why don't a few of us go grocery shopping, and we'll make dinner together instead?" I breathed a sigh of relief.

Sometimes we have to listen to our gut, our inner sense of knowing that tells us when a situation crosses the line from uncomfortable to dangerous. Our lines won't all be the same. I had a personal rule that when traveling for these retreats, I needed a toilet to be present. It isn't so much that I can't pee in the woods as much as the amenities available gave me a certain comfort that I could get to safety if I needed to. You might love camping, and if that's the case maybe your rule is that you need permission to have your cell phone so you can call if anything dramatic happens. Create the rules you need. Your safety matters and you shouldn't need receipts to be believed.

THE MARATHON

———

I suspect a lot of Black girls in white environments still endure awkward moments over their hair. It may happen when a coach decides everyone has to wear a "high pony" for team pictures. It could come in the form of questions from friends who don't realize our hair did not grow six inches overnight; it's just a blow out or some weave. And of course, many of us have dodged the inquisitive hands of white people who are desperate to touch our hair as if we are some kind of pet. I have a friend who was recently asked by another adult whether she has to wash her hair or if it's always dirty. Ridiculous.

It's frustrating because, while we know so much about white people, they are required to know so little about us. We know which aisles contain hair products for them. We know how it starts to look oily and stringy if they haven't washed it recently. We know which hair tools were made with their hair texture in mind. But they don't know about twist outs and shrinkage. They don't understand that washing our hair could require an entire day. They call our hair styles "inappropriate" or "unprofessional." That is, until a celebrity or fashion designer wants to rock them. Even when they try to copy our styles like cornrows or dreadlocks, it just doesn't compare to what our hair can do.

I struggled with my hair when I was a kid. I had a relaxer, but most of the time, one of my parents did it over the kitchen sink. And just in case you don't know much about relaxers, let me say this: Relaxers are a cocktail of chemicals that can straighten your hair. Typically, you then need a touch-up every six to eight weeks to straighten any new growth. But the chemicals are so strong, if you leave them on your head too long, they can cause your hair to break or even burn your scalp. Believe me, I know.

Because of those over-the-kitchen-sink relaxers and my overuse of a flat iron, my hair was broken off and uneven. In some spots, it was still thick and kinky at the root; in other spots, it lay flat. My hair never achieved the same looks as the girls on the Just for Me box.

On top of these hair woes, the adults in my life were obsessed with what they called "bumping the ends of my hair." But, y'all, this was no slight curl. These curls had my shoulder-length hair up by my earlobes! I spent a lot of my preteen time in the mirror, trying desperately to comb out the curls in an attempt to make myself look thirteen, instead of seven.

Every summer my dad would take the time to corn-row my hair. It was always so sweet. My dad, standing over me, meticulously parting every row. I could hear the click of his large fingernails bumping into one another as he worked. Every time I sat down, I hoped I would emerge looking like Brandy or Alicia Keys. (They rocked braids hard in the '90s and stayed fly.) What I didn't know was that most girls my age—and the celebrities I admired—added extensions to their braids. That's why they were thick and long. But my dad was not adding extensions to mine. Every time I got out of the chair, after hours of sitting, my braids were wonky and uneven.

Thankfully my friends never made fun of me. I think they knew my hair was not being done at a salon, and I was doing the best I could. Still I longed, just once, to walk into school and hear another Black girl say, "Ohhh, that's so cute. Imma get my hair done like that next week." You know?

When I turned sixteen, everything changed. My mom found a braider. I gathered everything I would need and hauled it into my grandmother's basement—

soft pillows so I could sit on the floor, a pile of movies I wouldn't actually be able to see but could maybe hear, a blow dryer, a couple of combs, and a lighter (back then we burned the ends of our braids instead of putting them in water to seal them). What I forgot, because it was my first time, was the Advil.

Nonetheless, I sat patiently as she finished the first row at the back of my head, and then a second and a third. After the first movie went off, I reached back to feel how far she had gotten. I was thrilled! She had done a lot in such a short time. For a moment I thought, *Maybe this won't take as long as I thought.* I thought wrong.

When the second movie went off, my head was still bent at an angle. My neck hurt. My back hurt. And I couldn't figure out why I felt so sleepy—she was doing all the work! Every now and then we took a break, so we could both stretch and wake ourselves up. We wiggled and did little dances—anything to boost our energy.

In went the third movie. It was just noise in the background. Neither of us could focus on what was happening. I had hair all in my face as she pushed the remaining hair around my head to see her parts. She was staring intently at my scalp and her handiwork, making sure everything stayed uniform. We both kept moving our butts around our seats, desperately searching for the right amount of pressure that would relieve the ache and allow us to keep going.

That movie ended. She said the magic words, "We are almost finished." What I didn't know is that "almost finished" meant we were definitely more than halfway through. It was okay. Her words gave me the hope I needed to endure the neck cramps and just believe that we would finish before dawn. Her fingers moved so fast down each braid. I could feel my hair tightening against my scalp with every section she finished.

By hour eight, I was no longer sure I was gonna make it. Was it rude to fall asleep while someone is trying to give you the look you desire? It seemed rude. I rolled my back. I asked for one more break. We both went to the restroom. Then we stood and looked at each other, trying to find our last bit of strength to get the job done.

"Ready?" she asked.

"Ready," I responded.

Finally at hour 9 or 10, when I could barely keep my eyes open anymore and could no longer feel my legs, she announced, "Finished."

I turned around, to look up at her. "Really?" I asked.

She smiled down at me, "Really! Go ahead and feel it."

I did. I ran my hands over my scalp, where I could now feel the braids between my fingers. I looked down at my shoulders and noticed how the braids fell forward, allowing me to flip them back.

I tried my best to be polite, thanking her graciously, helping her clean up, and seeing her to the door after my mom paid her. I'm not sure I even closed the front door before I was racing to the bathroom mirror. And couldn't nobody tell me nothin'! My braids were halfway down my back—long and luscious. They formed their own little perfect checkerboard across my scalp, showing off the parted perfection. I swung them from side to side. Pretended to put them half up and half down. Flipped my head upside down and gathered them all at the top, allowing just a couple of strands to hang down as if they'd just happened to fall in my face.

For the first time I was ecstatic about my hair, about what it could do . . . about how another Black girl, only a few years older than me, had given up her evening to help me feel like *this*.

After that I became a lot more adventurous with my hair. I colored it. I cut it. I went natural. I got another relaxer. Went natural again. I basically have a whole hair store in my house from trying to figure out the right products and the right tools for each of those seasons. Learning to love my hair and what it can do has been a journey, but one I appreciate.

My little sister, who was only six years old that first

time I got braids, is now my sister stylist. Every few weeks, I sit between her legs as her fingers dance through my hair. She encourages me to keep taking risks with my hair. She eases any anxiety I may be feeling and always makes sure I'm happy with how it turns out. She is patient and kind. I love engaging in this sacred Black girl ritual with her.

I have fallen in love with my hair, but it took time, and it all started with a Black girl basement braiding marathon.

FIRST LOVE

<hr />

Just a few weeks after my braiding marathon, I was headed back to my grandmother's house. It was summer, but my brother and I had long outgrown the need for summer day camp. We spent most of our days recording music off the radio, reading endless piles of books, or watching daytime talk shows and soap operas. So my mother decided to scoop us up and get us out of the house for a bit.

As we wound through the neighborhood, we came upon the house of my mom's friend Mrs. Jackson. My mom noticed the cars in the driveway, and I asked her how long it had been since she had seen her friend. "Long time," she responded. The pair had been best friends since high school, and I could tell by the look on her face that she wanted to stop. I nodded at her before she asked her question. "Yeah, we can stop, Momma." I figured if I got bored, I could walk to my grandmother's house; she lived two streets over. Besides it was fun to watch my mom with her longtime friend. I enjoyed seeing her come alive that way.

What I did not expect was Ryan, the gorgeous sixteen-year-old boy who opened the door. The last time I saw Ryan, I was probably eleven. He was obsessed with basketball, often stealing my brother outside to play a couple of games in the driveway. I was happy to lay under our mothers' feet reading *Highlights* magazines. Born only months apart, we had known each other our entire lives, so we were never offended by each other's disinterest. But now . . .

His big brown eyes were as deep as ever, shining under his thick Black hair. His athletic build was obvious—he clearly played ball, and not just in the driveway anymore. His skin glowed, the same golden bronze as his mom's. He smiled as he let us in, and I thought I might melt into a puddle right there in that living room I had visited more times than I could count. I begged my knees to cooperate and keep walking.

Our mothers disappeared into the kitchen. Our little brothers ran off to the den. Ryan invited me to watch TV in the living room. We talked as long as our moms did. Our curiosity about each other must have been radiating through the entire house. Gone were the little kids who were polite but uninterested. In their place now sat two teenagers who were *very interested.* The TV was on, but Ryan never once glanced over at it. He looked straight into my eyes, asking me all kinds of questions about my hobbies, likes, and dislikes.

Before leaving, he asked if we could see a movie together. He didn't hesitate—strong, confident, but also eager, hopeful.

My heart leaped. "Sure, I'd like that," I said. We made a plan before I headed to the car. Who imagined my first date would be with someone I'd known my entire life? I looked at my mom in the car and squealed.

On the day of our date, Ryan and his dad arrived at exactly 7:00 P.M. Neither of us had a driver's license, so it was Mr. Jackson behind the wheel. Ryan came to the door to collect me, and we both slid into the backseat.

My still fresh braids were pulled into a ponytail on top of my head. (Had to make those cheekbones pop!) I had on my favorite blue-jean skirt with an asymmetrical cut. My T-shirt was baby blue and made my chest look far more significant than it actually was. I wasn't really into makeup, but I'd stolen a bit from my mom for the occasion.

Ryan had on a pair of jeans and a T-shirt. His hair was a perfect 'fro. I thought his cologne might intoxicate me. *Was it hot in here, or is it just summer?* I wasn't sure.

On the way to the theater, his father asked lots of questions. What movie were we going to see? What time did it start? How long would it last? Did we have quarters for the pay phone? All the questions parents had to ask before the internet and cellphones.

Once we arrived, his father turned to the backseat with instructions. "Ryan, when the movie is over, use the pay phone to call me. I will come pick you up. Do not walk home, Ry."

Ryan opened his hand and showed him the change he was carrying. "I got it," he replied. Then he turned to me: "Ready?" I'm pretty sure my smile was the only answer he needed.

I remember nothing about the movie . . . only that I couldn't believe I was on a real date. When the movie ended, we sat and talked until we got kicked out because the staff needed to clean before the next showing. We walked slowly to the lobby. It was weirdly wonderful to know Ryan so well and still need all the details filled in. I knew about his family and where he lived. I knew what grade he was in (same as me since forever). I knew he loved sports, especially basketball. But I didn't know the details. How else did he spend his time when not playing ball? How close was he to his little brother? What was his school like? I suddenly wanted every detail I could get.

Turns out, so did he.

Once we were in the lobby, we walked over to the pay phones, but he never picked one up. He stared at me, saying nothing for a moment. I looked at him quizzically as I watched his brain hatching a plan. Finally, he spoke: "I don't want this to end yet. I know my dad said to call, but I'd really like to walk you home." He was going to defy his parents.

I asked him if he was sure, but I didn't really need to. I could see it in his face. He was not picking up that phone unless I asked him to—and I was not going to do that. I wanted every moment I could get.

We left the theater on foot.

Outside the air was much warmer than the air-conditioned theater we'd just left. As we walked home, the remnants of smoke hung in the air—the perfect mix of barbecue fires that had ended and home fireworks that had already popped. The smell of summer. The sky was empty of clouds but full of stars. We looked up every time our conversation drifted into a comfortable silence.

As we walked in and out of the shadows cast by streetlights, we talked about my parents' divorce and all that had happened in its wake. We talked about our favorite music and TV shows. We talked about who we were in school and who we wished we could be. We told each other the truth. We laughed hard and loudly. Not exactly strangers, we easily moved into friendship, trust, vulnerability. We drank each other in.

At the end of the night, he hugged me goodbye, lifting my feet off the ground. He knew he needed to race home at this point. I could tell he didn't want to go. He made me promise we would see each other again soon.

I floated into the house. Did all that really just happen to *me*? Everyone was asleep, and I was glad. I didn't want to try to translate all my feelings into words. I wanted to explore all the nooks and crannies of this new feeling alone. I longed to remember the shape of it, the feel of falling in love. I fell asleep replaying the entire night in my head.

The next morning the house phone rang. My grandmother said it was for me. I never got phone calls at her house, so I knew it had to be Ryan. My heart started racing.

When I answered the phone, it wasn't him. It was his mom.

"Hello, Austin," she began. "As you know, Ryan was given specific instructions last night to call us to come pick you all up from the theater. Since he did not do that, he is now on punishment. But before that punishment begins, he has made a request to talk with you. I am giving him five minutes, and I will be standing right here." With that, she handed him the phone.

"Austin, I want you to know that I had a wonderful time with you last night. As my mom said, I'm on punishment now, so I won't be able to call you for a few days. But I didn't want you to wonder if something was wrong. In fact, I want you to know that being put on punishment was entirely worth our evening together. If I had to do it all over again, I wouldn't change a thing. I'll call you as soon as I can. Okay?"

I whispered, "Okay," my breath taken away realizing what he'd just said in front of his mom while on punishment. I let out a surprise giggle as I hung up the phone and turned to my mom, who had entered the room. It wasn't a dream. It wasn't a movie. I'd had one perfect date, and I was in love.

The relationship lasted for about three seconds. Why? Because it was a long-distance relationship. For the first time in my life, I had found someone that I clicked with—and I had to look *waaay* outside my school to find him. It was a lovely relationship. But without all the advantages of today's technology, it just couldn't be sustained.

As a Black girl who personally prioritized a shared racial identity, attending predominately white schools wasn't doing me any favors in the dating department. There just weren't many options at any school I attended. And truth be told, it can be easy to feel invisible or awkward or self-conscious as a Black girl in a predominately white school. I spent most of my high school and college careers watching others fall in and out of love. My crew was my girls and, honestly, that was a different kind of amazing.

I had a blast with my friends. We celebrated our birthdays together, traveled together, and created our own spa nights when we were feeling stressed. We took walks in the park, perused the art museum, and made sure to attend the Christmas lighting at the zoo. Our movie nights were delightful. We went to most school dances as a group. We got all dressed up, took ourselves out to dinner, and stayed up all night afterward discussing the evening's drama. On Valentine's Day, we would have what my friend Manesha called "ro'tic nights" (*romantic* without the *man,* because we either didn't have a man or didn't want one—ha!). We gave ourselves decadent chocolate chip cookies and poured sparkling grape juice into champagne glasses. We bought flowers and strung up fairy lights. We shared vulnerably and laughed until our cheeks hurt.

As we grew older and each moved in and out of dating relationships, we were there for one another. Sharing inside jokes. Crying into one another's laps. Taking epic road trips. We've been together through breakups, family fallouts, painful losses, and magical celebrations. We've healed side by side. We've even dodged tornadoes together—literally! While there are some romantic relationships I question in hindsight, there is not one day that I spent with my friends that I want to take back.

I thought my first love was Ryan, but the truth is my first love has been my girls.

REPRESENT

—————

My grandmother is my hero. I never really intend for her to swoop in and rescue me, but that's often how it turns out. G. Jacqueline Austin was born in 1931 in a coal miners' town. Because both her parents were educators, they soon made their way to a Black neighborhood in Beckley, West Virginia, in need of teachers and principals. There the family thrived. They built their own house, led a number of social organizations, and regularly were praised in the "colored" section of the newspaper for being leaders in the community. After high school, my grandmother attended an HBCU (of course, then it was a "colored" college) and became a member of the AKA sorority, a title she still proudly wears into her nineties. After meeting my grandfather, the pair moved to Cleveland, Ohio, and eventually settled in a suburb, Warrensville Heights, where they would raise their family. She would continue to call it home for at least forty years.

By the time I finished my senior year of high school, my mom had moved from Cleveland to another state. I was supposed to spend the summer with her but I didn't want to spend my last summer before college indoors, in a town I didn't know, with no friends. I complained to my grandmother, having no expectation of her solving my little crisis. But that's exactly what she did. Somehow this woman snagged me a paid internship working for the local government of Warrensville Heights. I would live with her for the summer.

When I went to fill out the paperwork for my new job, I met a number of teenagers who would be working for the city, too. Many of them were planning to work outside at parks and recreation or lifeguard at the local pools. My grandmother, on the other hand, had pulled some major strings. I discovered that I would be working in the mayor's office in city hall.

I was anxious on my first day. I wore a long maxi skirt and breezy top to make sure my thighs and armpits could get some air as I sweated from nervousness and heat. When I stepped into the building, I gasped. There were Black women everywhere. All summer I felt like I was dreaming as I watched them run the city. The mayor, Marcia L. Fudge, stayed busy. She was smart, direct, and determined to be fully present for her city. Every morning, she would hand me a newspaper with one article circled. By lunchtime, she'd pop over to my makeshift desk and ask me what I thought about the article. She pushed me to connect the dots between what I was reading in the paper and the work being done in the building. I felt honored that she would invest her time in me, despite her extraordinarily busy schedule. She made me feel like she was preparing me for something great, something even I couldn't predict. My supervisor was Linda, a tall, thin, dark-skinned woman who was full of life. Her energy was boundless but never overwhelming. She raced around that building all day every day, prioritizing tasks for the mayor, handling anything that didn't require the mayor's attention, and generally keeping the office from falling into disarray. It was a sight to behold.

When all the women went on break, I had to step up to the plate and handle the phone lines. Usually those were managed by Veronica, a thick Black woman, often draped in animal print, with a voice that would calm down the Hulk. When she spoke, you felt like everything was going to work out. My teenage angst needed her in my life. But even Veronica needed to give her voice a break. So when she went to lunch with the other women, it was my turn to take over. I felt like a true member of the team when I could answer residents' questions instead of calling them back after I learned the answer. I felt special working for them—the staff and the residents. Of course, I refused to stay in my little corner of city hall. Before I knew it, I was also hanging out with Barbara Walker, the chief of staff, who regaled me with stories from her own life and the life of her sister, Congresswoman Stephanie Tubbs Jones. I hovered over the shoulders of the Community Development and Finance Directors Brad and Ferris as they pored over architect plans, and then joined them in walking the grounds where proposed buildings might one day stand. I handed out T-shirts to local Little League teams with Rob. Every day was new and different. Every day I sat under the leadership of these incredible Black leaders—watching them turn a city into a community.

My absolute favorite project was working on a community-wide end-of-summer bash. We took over the largest park in town and set up bouncy houses, games, beer gardens (which, of course, I was not allowed to double-check). All day, I was everyone's assistant. I don't know that I was helpful at all, but I was sincere in my desire to make sure the day went off without a hitch. It was an incredible way to end the summer surrounded by my mentors, the sun setting over the city I had fallen in love with, the shouts of children and families having fun. But the greatest gift I received can be summed up in a word our society is using a lot these days: representation. In my world, where I had never had a Black teacher other than my choir director, this was the opportunity that would change me from the inside out.

As summer came to a close, so did my high school career and my time at home. I was bound for North Park University in Chicago and would carry this experience with me.

INDIGNITIES

The older I got, the more I started to recognize the small indignities we faced on a regular basis—from overt racism, like being called the N-word, to teachers silently assuming the worst of us. By the time I was in college, my patience was running thin.

North Park's campus sat in the middle of an incredibly diverse neighborhood, Albany Park—but the school itself was still predominantly white. I arrived on campus early for a program called Kuumba—a chance for students of color to meet and connect. For those first few weeks, we felt like we owned the campus . . . until all the other students arrived. That was when we quickly realized how the school's Swedish history would soon impact us.

On the first official day of school, I was sitting on the far left side of a classroom watching my peers walk through the door. I was the only Black girl among the students, so I was thrilled when my friend Will appeared in the doorway. I watched him scan the room for a familiar face and smile when he saw me. He swung his backpack on one shoulder, sauntered over, and slid into the seat next to me.

Once all of us were seated, our teacher introduced herself and then announced we would open with an icebreaker. Each student would state the name they'd like to be called during class and share where in the world their family was from.

Everyone nodded enthusiastically—everyone except us, the two Black students.

Will gently kicked me. I reached over to his desk and drew a little heart on his notebook with my left hand.

We didn't look at each other. We didn't say anything. And yet we were having a whole conversation, our shared Black identity uniting us.

We turned our attention to the other students and listened as their responses snaked around the room. Some kids gave straightforward answers like Sweden or England. Some called themselves "a mutt" before listing four or five countries where their relatives were from. But everyone seemed to have an answer to this question. Will and I knew we didn't.

The responses kept coming, each one causing a

twinge of pain. We weren't upset that everyone else knew their family's origins. We were disappointed because no one realized there were two people who didn't. And no one thought to have a conversation about why that was.

I had been silently debating what I would do when it came time for Will and me to respond—we were the last two students who would have to introduce ourselves and explain our family's history. Soon I was out of time.

I answered, "My name is Austin, and my family is from (*dramatic pause*) Georgia."

Then Will introduced himself and added, "My family is from Africa. All of Africa. Just . . . the whole thing." He held up both hands, spreading his fingers wide for emphasis.

For the first time since class began, we actually looked at each other, and before we knew it was going to happen, we burst into laughter. I mean we laughed HARD.

Thirty people in a classroom, and we were the only two who couldn't answer a simple question about family origin because of a major series of events that had shaped our family trees. Thanks to the Middle Passage and centuries of enslavement that ripped apart Black families like ours, "Georgia" and "Africa" were the best answers we could give—but they were also woefully incomplete.

Will and I were expected to keep it all to ourselves and let the class move on.

Except we couldn't. It was too absurd. So, we laughed at the absurdity. And then we apologized for our laughter. But that set off a new round of laughter. I was laughing so hard I had to wipe tears away.

On the day of that icebreaker, I needed to laugh until my eyes watered. I don't fully know why. Maybe it was because I believed that was the safest way to cry. Or maybe my body was rejecting my teacher's silence on American history and the normalization of an activity that clearly left some of us out.

I don't think my teacher intended for me and Will to feel left out. I don't think she intended to hurt our feelings. I don't think she was trying to be mean. I think she was proud of her family's origin story and thought it would be fun for students to be able to share theirs as well. But her intention didn't prevent Will and me from feeling hurt and left out.

Once it was out there, Will and I had to make a decision. Would we accept this moment or reject it?

With our overly simplistic answers, our laughter, and our silent communication, we rejected the indignity of not having an answer that every other student in our class did. And we reclaimed our dignity, our self-worth. It was one of the first times I gave myself permission to cause a disruption.

Of course, it wouldn't be the last time I'd face insensitivity in the classroom. When faced with other indignities, my responses varied. I sometimes excused myself to use the restroom, taking the opportunity to walk off my frustration. When feeling insulted, I might raise my hand and interrupt what I was supposed to ignore. Other times I would offer a hard-edged response to my professor, daring them to give me an opportunity to really speak my mind. I vented with friends and complained to my parents. And when I was angry enough that I had to do something more, I'd write a letter to the school's administration or join a community fighting back. Different situations required different responses, but after that day with Will, I learned to always listen to my body. Little did I know, I was headed straight into a situation that helped me define myself as a disrupter.

THE TRIP

Going to college in Chicago was amazing. I had my first homecoming dance in the lion's den at the Lincoln Park Zoo. When we wanted new posters, we traveled to the Boystown neighborhood. If we felt like shopping, we'd hop on the L and head to Mag Mile. There were a million coffee shops where we could work or chat and an abundance of restaurants to try. The city was our playground. But we also took advantage of the many programs our school offered to travel outside the city. One of those was called Sankofa. This was an opportunity to learn more about the racial history of America. And that year, the trip included a stop at a former plantation.

We traveled for fourteen hours to get there. By the time we tumbled off the bus, we were sleepy and cranky, but also relieved to finally be at our destination. Once our feet hit the ground, we tried to unfold ourselves, stretching as far as our limbs would reach while we eyed our new surroundings.

The view was mostly a wide-open white cotton field. Several small cabins dotted the landscape. One battered two-story building loomed in the distance as if it were watching all of us.

The tour began in a dark one-room church. We dutifully sat on worn, knotted benches as our eyes roamed over every crevice of the building. Had any of the enslaved people sat right where I was sitting now? Had they turned their faces toward these same windows and imagined freedom beyond the cotton field? I wasn't really listening to the video that played on the large screen in front of us. I was wondering if the sweat of my Black ancestors had seeped into the wood where I sat.

My attention shifted when the video ended and a white woman in full 1800s garb stepped forward. She wanted us to know that the plantation had been in her family for generations, and they were proud of its history. This made me suspicious. "Proud of the plantation's history" didn't sound enough like "devastated by our ancestors' participation in this horrendous practice of human torture" for me. I sat quietly and squinted at her, trying to keep my peace and offer her the benefit of the doubt. Maybe my interpretation of her words wasn't quite what she meant.

Another tour guide joined her, and the pair split us into two groups. My group went to the next stop on the tour—one of the shabby cabins where enslaved families had made an attempt at having a private life. The tour guide pointed out that the slaves on this plantation had been happy to be here because the owners were kind. "Many owners didn't provide things like this." She waved her hand over a trough on the floor. "And the slaves were so smart, they made everything serve double duty. Sometimes this was where food was held, but other times it became a crib for the babies." She smiled. I did not.

I couldn't help but imagine the lives of the people who once lived in this place. I looked at the pallets on the floor. No way they provided comfort after hours upon hours of laboring in the field. My eyes climbed the walls up to the shingled roof. It wasn't hard to imagine how the wind would whistle, or the rain would seep, or the sun would burn through the cracks. Whatever the weather was doing outside surely also happened inside this bark-covered cabin. There was nothing kind about treating people this way. It was cruel.

We then followed the tour guide to what she called the sewing room. When I entered I saw a large quilt prominently displayed over a piece of furniture. The tour guide beamed. "Slaves made such beautiful things in here. Of course, they had to do some regular sewing for the mistresses, but that didn't stop them from creating some of the most beautifully patterned quilts." I was captured by this quilt, flapping against whatever lay beneath. I desperately wanted to touch it, smell it, to whisper apologies into its woven fibers. The discordance between my own thoughts and the chirpy attitude of the tour guide was becoming too much to bear.

The tour concluded at the edge of the cotton field. We stood in the shadow of the two-story building, which I learned was the cotton gin. It wasn't lost on me that the gin had two balconies overlooking the field. The plants stretched on and on and on. The two tour guides were now together, sharing their grandmother's memories of how happy the slaves had been while laboring in the field. "They sang the most beautiful songs," one recalled her grandmother saying, before listing how many bales of cotton the slaves were expected to pick each day.

We couldn't take it anymore. The Black students started firing questions at the guides, the heat in our voices unmistakable.

"Did the enslaved people ever hurt themselves while picking all this cotton?"

"Was punishment ever doled out for not picking enough?"

"What were the lives of the enslaved children like? Did they get to play games and run around like the enslaver's children?"

Our questions weren't sincere. We knew the answers; we just wanted to poke holes in their ridiculous assumptions about the inner lives of the enslaved.

But the guides just gawked at us. They seemed genuinely confused about why we were so upset. "Listen, guys," one of them said, "the tour is over, but we have one more special surprise for you!" We stopped our questions. "You all are now welcome to grab a sack and go pick some cotton!"

There was a collective pause, then a thunderclap of explosion, as multiple Black students exclaimed, "What?!" in complete disbelief. I was disgusted by the entire framing of the tour. In that moment, which felt like the pinnacle of disrespect toward the enslaved and the history the tour guides were responsible for sharing, I could have lit that whole field on fire. I wasn't the only one. Some of my friends were stunned into silence, not moving a muscle as they glared at the guides in their hoopskirts. But a handful of students around me shouted at them. I was nervous one or two would completely lose it, so I started dragging my friends away. The last thing we needed was an assault charge here.

Tension hung in the air as we all climbed back on the

bus. Black students and white students went back and forth, in a swirling conversation that felt as disconnected as the tour guides were from history. I was disgusted by the cheerfulness being used to teach about the legacy of slavery in America.

I could feel the anger churning inside me. It was no longer an indecipherable blob. It was forming into rage, and that rage hardened into conviction. As I listened to other students process what we had just experienced, my own thoughts felt like pieces of a puzzle snapping together for rebuttal or defense. My hands shook as I stood up to address everyone. But I wasn't afraid. On the contrary, I was resolute. I was bound and determined to correct the narrative, to say hard things, to tell the truth.

I spoke about my own reactions to walking this land, my anger about the framing of this tour, my anguish for the lives held in chains here. By the time I sat back down, a feeling of peace had washed over me. My anger hadn't destroyed me. It didn't leave me alone and isolated. I didn't feel bad or guilty or ashamed. My anger had given me the courage I needed to defend Black lives—even those of my ancestors. I no longer needed to fear myself. In a very real way, finally expressing it made me feel whole.

CRENDALYN

T hankfully, not everything in college was a racial battle. My first and biggest surprise when I set foot on campus was Crendalyn McMath. She was my marketing professor, and she was a Black woman—the first Black woman teacher I'd ever had.

Professor McMath took command of every classroom she stepped into. Tall, with shoulder-length black hair, she wore suits that seemed only to elongate her frame. She was a brilliant teacher who brought stories from corporate America into the classroom.

The gift of Professor McMath's presence went beyond the fact that she looked like me, though that was special all by itself. The true gift was that I didn't have to create my own sense of belonging in her class. In every previous classroom, I had been responsible for decoding teachers' references to experiences I wasn't familiar with:

It's like when you're sailing . . . or *You know how when you're camping, you have to . . .*

Many of my white teachers were committed to the belief that *we are all the same,* a good idea on paper. But in practice it meant that teachers often assumed we all experience the world in the same ways. For example, once a teacher wanted to drive home the point that we should do something daily. She likened it to how you wash your hair every morning. I don't think it ever occurred to her that none of the Black students washed their hair every day . . . and shouldn't!

When moments like this happened, Black kids would nod politely, rarely correcting these assumptions. Our teachers' belief that their experiences were universal (meaning they applied to everyone) kept them from being aware of other cultures, other realities, other truths. Honestly, we didn't mind keeping our culture under wraps. And besides, who had time to teach the teacher?

But Professor McMath was different. One day while illustrating a point regarding business planning, she decided to use the example of opening a beauty shop. She asked us to name how much we would charge a client for a cut, color, shampoo, etc. Our conversation moved along as usual until she referred to the costs of getting a relaxer. My head snapped up in recognition, while all the white students looked completely baffled. I was the only Black student in the class and the only one who understood the reference. I smiled at Professor McMath, while she feigned surprise at the other students' confusion: "Come on, you all. You know what a relaxer is, right?"

The other students continued to stare blankly at her until she explained that, instead of wearing their hair natural, some Black women choose to get a relaxer, which is sort of the opposite of what happens when white people get a perm. "Relaxers make black curly hair straight. They relax the curls." She winked at me, and I grinned from ear to ear.

As I looked around the room, I thought to myself, *Wow, I am actually included in the example being presented. This is what it's like to not have to reinterpret, to not have to smile and nod.*

In any other class, I knew if I had written about getting a relaxer, the teacher would have circled the word and drawn a question mark above it, asking if that was the word I meant to use, or else they would have crossed it out altogether and written "I don't know what this word is." I had spent my entire education doing the work to make sure I wasn't misinterpreted by my own teachers. But here, I was finally understood.

Professor McMath hugely impacted my education.

She was a wonderful professor whose teachings I still carry with me. But she also gave me something more. Because of her classroom, I didn't feel like I was attending a school made for other students. I belonged, just like everyone else.

It felt wonderful, as though a whole world of possibilities had opened up to me. And in a real way, they had. I learned to expect more.

BELONGING

———

The first time I walked across the open space of my college campus I almost got knocked out by a flying neon green Frisbee. I had not seen a Frisbee since I was a little kid, so I had no expectation that I'd need to be on the lookout for one while walking in Chicago. Nonetheless, there I was, ducking for cover.

Ultimate Frisbee, acoustic guitars, lying in the grass to tan, regularly leaving the city to go camping—these were things I thought happened only in books and movies. But at my school, I was the odd one for not participating.

There was one tradition, however, I didn't have a choice about participating in. At the beginning of every spring semester—no matter what classroom you were in—the professor would stop teaching ten minutes before class ended, take out a list, and begin reading the names on it, asking anyone whose name was called to raise their hand. Most of the time it was students of color who had their hands in the air. The professor would then inform us that we were behind on tuition payments and had a certain number of days to "rectify the situation."

The first time this happened, I couldn't believe our personal information was made public like that. By the second and third time, the other students and I were raising our hands before our names were even called.

All of us with our hands in the air knew that even if we managed to secure scholarships or grant money, even if we held jobs and took out loans to cover what we couldn't pay, even if we negotiated our way back into the classroom through the financial aid office, we were still scraping by.

Truth is, my family wasn't poor. But every school I attended was a private school, which meant you had to pay big money to attend. My parents made it happen, but it wasn't easy. Every dime they had went toward our education—and occasionally there wasn't enough money left for things like . . . electricity.

So I was very familiar with the folks who worked in the financial aid office, but I also noticed that some of my classmates had their last names etched into the sides of buildings on campus. Between this and ducking Frisbees, I realized the school probably wasn't built with me in mind.

While working on this chapter, I spent an hour looking up the racial histories of the schools I attended. Surprise! Despite plenty of details about their "proud legacies," not one of them has a paragraph on when they decided to integrate or what happened when the first Black students were admitted. Most of them skip right over the era of integration and instead focus on when the first Black someone did something notable—the first Black professor was hired, the first Black student union was established, the first Black homecoming queen or valedictorian or principal was named.

But it's fairly easy to fill in the blanks with American history. We know that America initially forbade Black people to be educated by making it illegal for enslaved persons to learn to read or write. When slavery was abolished, segregation became the law of the land, forcing white students and Black students to attend separate schools. Black schools were significantly underfunded, but not because the Black community was indifferent about education. A web of racist policies was responsible for significantly lowering the amount of money available to fund Black schools.

When the Supreme Court of the United States finally acknowledged that having white schools and Black schools was inherently unequal, integration orders followed for public schools across America. Do you know what became popular after integration orders were set in motion? Private schools, where white people could legally deny admission to Black students.

My point is that because America has such a long and horrendous history of unequal education, you should feel no shame or embarrassment over what it takes to complete yours. Whether you got there through affirmative action, scholarships, grants, scraping by, working, or some combination of the above, you deserve a rich and meaningful education. No professor with a list of past-due payments can change that fact.

My first time really addressing my own sense of belonging came when an article appeared in our student paper. It was an opinion piece saying that all the students who complained that our school wasn't diverse enough should just leave, since we obviously didn't like it here.

I didn't respond by writing back to the paper, but trust and believe I used my voice anytime the article was brought up inside or outside the classroom. The moment I was accepted as a student, I belonged. That was it, and that was enough. That was my permission slip to make my needs and wants and desires known.

Lots of other students of color felt the same way. We banded together. We worked to change the musical selections for our chapel services. Because of our work, gospel songs and songs in other languages became normal to hear every week. When the school seemed like it was going to backpedal on some of its hiring commitments, we called a meeting with the administration to demand answers. We fought for funding for the programs that mattered to us.

One of my favorite actions that took place didn't involve me at all. Our school had an art gallery that most of us had to pass through on our way to classes. The art was constantly changing, and we were surprised to find that one day all the art pieces were depictions of Jesus . . . and every one of them was white. When we asked the administration about this choice, we were told, "It's just artistic expression," and the installation would remain as it was. The next day, I walked through the installation and discovered on the floor, underneath every art piece, was a new addition—a depiction of Jesus as a person of color.

Apparently, my friend Jackie made a trip to the computer room, printed off more diverse depictions of Jesus, and put them up without anyone's permission as her "artistic expression." It was genius.

Our school may have been historically Swedish, but it wasn't anymore. We were students who demanded an equal education, and for us that didn't just mean admittance—that meant having our needs met, too.

WHOSE FOREFATHERS?

Despite all my racial justice work on campus, somewhere along the way, I picked up the unspoken belief that I was made for white people. Much of my teaching (and learning) revolved around white people because those were the students (or professors or administrators) who needed my help to change their hearts and minds. Therefore, a good portion of my work included conversations about white privilege, white ignorance, white shame, and the things white people "needed" in order to believe that pursuing racial justice is a worthy cause.

I worked as if white folks were at the center, the great hope, the key to racial justice. I contorted myself to be a voice that white people could hear. It's amazing how white supremacy can invade even the programs aimed at destroying it! Just when I was about to lose myself to whiteness in an entirely different way, along came Dr. Rupe Simms.

Dr. Simms taught courses in African American and Mexican American history. Brown, bald, and bespectacled, he wore clothes from Phat Farm and had a small leather pouch that he strapped like a messenger bag across the front of his chest. Standing no taller than five foot seven, he nonetheless had a certain gravitas many students found intimidating. The man was an intellectual powerhouse with a wealth of experience that kept him grounded in real life. Many of the white students avoided his courses like the plague, but I didn't know a Black student who would dare graduate without taking at least one of his classes. Dr. Simms believed in the power of Black history and Black culture. He believed it could change our lives.

Dr. Simms was right.

He began each class period with a list of terms written on the chalkboard—one of which was usually spelled incorrectly. We often teased him for being so brilliant that he didn't have space in his brain for such trivial matters as spelling. For a class period focusing on slavery in America, we would arrive with Dr. Simms's terms already on the board: *chattel, Middle Passage, slave codes, rebellion, Dred Scott,* and five or six more phrases. He would then spend the class defining each term as he weaved them into a story, making us feel like we were witnesses to events of the past.

As he taught, Dr. Simms spoke softly, often repeating himself, making sure we understood his point. But he also wanted to know what we thought. "Tell me, Kate, what do you think about that?" Dr. Simms would ask. If someone spoke too quietly or too hesitantly, he would extend his index and middle fingers together, twirling them in the air as he encouraged the student. "Speak up. Speak up. We want to hear what you have to say. Speak up so those in the back can hear you." It didn't matter whether our contributions were profound or basic—Dr. Simms always found a way to incorporate our ideas into his lecture. His gentleness did not stop him from demanding that we think deeply.

He also taught us to analyze current events, especially in the news. Did anyone notice how the faces of only the Black criminals were shown in this segment? In the next segment the anchor said there was a "large" crowd. Could you tell if the camera angle made it seem large or small? That whole story was on immigrants, but why did it focus only on immigrants of color? He wanted us to pay attention. He often brought newspapers to class—one the English-language *Chicago Tribune* and the other *Hoy*, the Spanish-language paper headquartered in the same city. He would have us read two stories on the same topic, then ask, "How are these two stories different? What details did the *Trib* leave out or *Hoy* include?"

He encouraged us to question everyday "patriotic" language. When referring to the drafters of the Constitution, for example, Dr. Simms refused to call them the Founding Fathers. "Those aren't my Fathers!" he would state matter-of-factly. His declaration invited the question for the rest of us: *Are they mine?*

His class was the first history course I took where I didn't have to quietly push back or whisper my resistance. I could be bold. I could say that the Constitution was an incredible document *and* that it has some significant problems. I could say that this country already had a foundation, and we needed to honor the Native peoples who cared for this land long before it was named the United States of America. I could analyze the gap between the statements of the Declaration of Independence and the existence of slavery. I could declare the truth about American history.

We always told Dr. Simms that he ruined our lives. He made us so aware of racial bias, we could no longer watch the news as leisure. We analyzed every news article with suspicion. We watched movies trying to determine both their accuracy and the point they were trying to convey. We thought critically about everything, and it was all Dr. Simms's fault.

He didn't just make us recite names and dates. He taught us to care about the past. When he spoke of Martin Luther King, Jr.'s assassination, his eyes would fill with tears. It was like he was hearing the announcement all over again. He wept so hard after showing us a documentary on the work of Cesar Chavez, he had to dismiss class early. He smiled wistfully as he recalled being mesmerized, glued to the sidewalk, while listening to Malcolm X speak in New York City. Dr. Simms wanted us to be emotionally connected to our learning, to sit in the pain and horror, but also the triumphs and achievements. He humanized the people who dared to stand against the system, and he made us believe that we could be part of that legacy of resistance. He told us that we, too, could be agents of change.

His course transformed me by setting me free. I didn't just have permission to tell the truth about history. I had permission to tell *my* truth. I had permission to make Black lives the center of my work. I had permission to be a disrupter, an agent of change. This got me into a ton of trouble in my jobs after graduation. But Dr. Simms had given me permission to speak up so those in the back could hear me. So I did.

DALIN

▬

Dear Dalin,

I think about you all the time.

You were always the fun one in the family. The one with the fastest jokes, the loudest laugh, and the best sense of style. We weren't super close—our eight-year age difference was probably to blame—but whenever we gathered as a family, I was drawn to you like a moth to Grandmommy's porch light.

You always seemed so cool and confident, like you knew you had the whole world in the palm of your hand. At least that's what I thought. I was so young then, and I didn't know what I didn't know. But when I saw your face twisted with anger and heard the fear in your voice that night, I understood what it must be like to be Black like you.

I had been sitting on the floor watching TV with

Grandmommy in her room, just happy to have her to myself in the small house filled with family gathered for the holiday.

We heard the commotion downstairs. *Bang!* the front door slammed shut behind you as voices started rising. Grandmommy and I could make out only snatches of words and phrases, but the one that stood out was the word *gun*. We looked at each other with eyes wide. She didn't move, so I didn't, either.

Minutes later you were standing in the doorway to her room. Your cool confidence had disappeared, replaced by anguish. "I was out with my friends when some dude took my shoes," you said, cracking your knuckles.

Grandmommy's confusion mirrored my own. "Took your shoes?" she asked.

You explained that you had just bought a new pair of sneakers and swapped out your old ones. After leaving the store, you and your friends were held up at gunpoint. You had no choice but to hand over the bright white shoes. And you were livid.

Still sitting on the floor, I stopped craning my neck to see your face and just stared at your feet. You had walked all the way home in just your socks.

"So what are you going to do now?" Grandmommy asked. She was clearly looking for an honest answer, and you didn't hesitate. "I'm looking for a gun to go get my shoes back," you said. Your knuckles cracked again.

I was instantly afraid. Even as a child, I knew it was your pride pushing you back out to the streets. And not the icky, arrogant kind. I mean the pride inherent in being human. The kind that flares when a stranger believes your life is worth less than a pair of sneakers. In your voice, I could hear the desire not quite for revenge but for the righting of a wrong. A desire to rearrange the world and go back to being in control, being safe, being in charge of what happened that night.

Even then I knew that going to the police wasn't a viable option for you. I quickly realized if I had been put in the same situation, I wouldn't have known where I could possibly get a gun. Yours was a world I knew only through headlines. So I believed your description of it. And I was afraid for you.

Our uncles stopped you from going back into the night, but the older you got, the more you had to navigate being a Black man in America on your own. In an overlooked and underresourced neighborhood like yours, getting pulled over by the police was a regular occurrence. I was horrified when I heard about how often police used those stops as an opportunity to harass and humiliate you.

As we grew older, both of us fell in love with words. You loved writing lyrics and pursued a rap career. I loved writing stories. My love for writing led me away from home to college. Your love for writing kept you in your neighborhood, intimately connected to your community. But by staying, you became inescapably intertwined with the criminal justice system.

By the time I left for college, you'd already had a number of run-ins with the courts. And when you received your third strike, the judge didn't have any options. A third offense meant a mandatory minimum of ten years in prison. Ten. Years.

Our family was stunned but determined to love you well. I think they did. But I wasn't sure how to.

For a long time I felt I shouldn't ask questions about your sentence or the circumstances of your arrest. I danced around it, trying to glean information without making anyone uncomfortable. I wish I had gotten over myself and just followed my heart. But because I didn't, it was years before I reached out.

Funny that we shared a love of writing, because it was a book that helped me overcome whatever fears I was harboring about reaching out to you. I read *A Place to Stand*, Jimmy Santiago Baca's bracing memoir of his life in prison. That book knocked the wind out of me.

As I read about the violence, the abuse, the humiliation, the evilness of the entire system, all I could think about was you.

I thought back to the night at Grandmommy's house: the violence you'd faced, the pressure you'd felt to defend yourself, and the obstacles you endured as you tried to build a life for yourself. Where were your options?

It was after reading *A Place to Stand* that I sent you a letter. I looked up your information. I researched all the rules I needed to follow. I wrote all three pages with the best penmanship I could muster. When I got to the end, I thought about including the words *I love you,* but I didn't. I thought you might laugh, might find those words offensive in light of my silence. I was so nervous, Dalin.

I wondered if the note would reach you. Then I wondered if you'd bother to respond, since I hadn't talked to you in years. I didn't know, but I had to try. I put it in the mail and waited. I waited so long, I almost missed your reply.

A month later the post office clerk set your letter on the counter in front of me. My hands trembled as I picked it up and walked to my car. I wondered if you wrote a one-word response or wrote longer just to tell me how disappointed you were that it took me so long to reach out. I opened the envelope. My eyes watered as I read the first line. "Yo, cuz. Yeah, I was surprised to get your letter, but we family so it's all love."

You responded to every question in my letter and shared about your life, your goals, your interests. The whole time I was reading I felt overwhelmed by grace. I was so excited to get to know you again.

I sat down and immediately started the next letter. But I don't know if you ever got it.

A few weeks later our whole family was together, celebrating Memorial Day, when we were told you'd died in prison. We were devastated. We still are.

During the wake, photos from your childhood scrolled across large screens, and I placed my hand on my Bible with your letter tucked in the front. To this day, it is a constant reminder of the man I know you were—funny, merciful, hopeful, connected to our family history, and wanting to come home. You were so many wonderful things that I wish the world had gotten to see. And I realized that everything you were was a direct result of where you came from.

For weeks after you died, I kept checking the mail, hoping for one more letter. One never came.

Now that you are gone, I often struggle with my anger. I'm angry that you didn't get to come home. I'm angry about the prison industrial complex that swept you up without care or concern. I'm angry at myself for not writing much, much sooner.

But I'm determined not to let that anger consume me. Instead, I have chosen to use it—because, Dalin, you should have been able to pursue writing and music, stay in your community, and still have plenty of options for your future. You should have been able to enjoy the gifts of your neighborhood instead of constantly weighing its systemic risks. You deserved a better America.

And I will do my best to call this nation to do better, to be better. I will shout that you were not the problem, that Black people, Black men, Black youth are not the problem. Injustice—how the good choices are reserved for only a few—is the problem.

I trust that you are safe now. I trust that you are surrounded by a peace that surpasses all understanding. And I hope that somewhere, someday, we'll sit down and write together.

I love you,
Austin

COMMUNITY

———

After college I went back to school to get a master's in social justice, which a lot of people thought was a terrible idea. I am still paying off the debt from this decision, but I have no regrets. Being challenged to think critically about varying intersections of justice movements, being in conversation with like-minded classmates who would push me and teach me . . . it was incredible. I loved being in the city of Detroit on Marygrove College's beautiful campus. Not only did it help me reconnect with Dalin, it also helped me build a solid foundation for becoming a writer and speaker long before I realized that would be my path.

And man, oh man, would I need that foundation as America's racial legacy came front and center.

I learned through documentaries that on Sunday,

September 15, 1963, a bomb tore through the walls of the 16th Street Baptist Church in Birmingham, Alabama. Inside, Black congregation members were preparing for their Sunday service, unaware that members of the Ku Klux Klan had laid sticks of dynamite under the church's stairs. Twenty-two people were injured in the attack, and four little girls were killed: Cynthia Wesley, Carole Robertson, and Addie Mae Collins—all fourteen years old—and eleven-year-old Denise McNair.

Just a couple of weeks earlier, Martin Luther King, Jr., had stood on the steps of the National Mall and given his famous "I Have a Dream" speech. In the following days, Alabama began integrating high schools and elementary schools for the first time in its history. The world was changing, and segregationists (those who didn't want integrated schools) could not contain their hatred and frustration. This was the third bombing in the eleven days since the integration order, but it was the first one to prove deadly.

The story of the four little girls was not covered in my elementary or high school history books. Those often limited the civil rights movement to three paragraphs and moved on. But my parents made sure I knew about this event. They showed me documentaries like *Eyes on the Prize* and Spike Lee's *4 Little Girls* to help me understand the context surrounding this horrendous bombing.

For me, and for many Black people, the story of the four little girls brings up strong emotions. Even Black folks who aren't religious understand the sacred role that churches have played in the life of the Black community. And back then, churches provided safety not only for spiritual nourishment but for political planning as well. Churches often served as meeting places for organizing. As a young person with a growing passion for justice and a love for church, I often wondered what might have been my fate had I been born in another place and time.

I stopped wondering when the distance between past and present closed on June 17, 2015. That day a white supremacist walked into Emanuel African Methodist Episcopal Church in Charleston, South Carolina, and took as many lives as he could with a handgun.

I was just about to turn over and go to sleep when I saw a tweet from an MSNBC anchor announcing that there had been a mass shooting in a Black church. My heart sank. The odds that the shooting wasn't racially motivated seemed impossible. I turned on the TV and watched the news for as long as I could stomach. My heart grew heavy as my eyes took it in. My beloved church had been attacked again.

I've never stepped inside Mother Emanuel, the loving nickname for that Charleston church. I don't know any of the congregation members, and I had never before heard the name of its beloved pastor or any of the people killed that night. And yet despite the geographical gap, it felt as if my own home church had been violated. The goal of terror, after all, is to inspire intimidation beyond the immediate target.

It worked. I was afraid.

When I teach about racism in America, I always leave time for questions. Though I travel all over the country, there are great similarities in the questions I receive. White people ask me how to be a better ally, sometimes even providing specific examples of where they've stumbled. Often white Christians will ask for help in understanding the connection between racial justice and the Bible. And sometimes the questions revolve around the latest national (or local) incident in which race is a hot topic due to tragedy, policy, or uproar.

And then there are questions Black people ask me. Black people ask me how to be confident in letting their children play outside. Black people ask me how to create safety on upcoming road trips that are causing more anxiety than excitement. Black people ask me how to handle the panic attacks that arise when passing police cars. Black people ask me what to do with their trauma, their stress, their fear. Black people ask me how to draw lines in the sand—how to stay informed but not retraumatize themselves, how to stay alert but not be afraid to go outside, how to process grief but without becoming despondent, how to fight back but not be consumed by rage.

Black people ask me fundamentally different questions because so many of us sense we are being stalked by the force, by the reality of racism. We know what it is to be afraid that something tragic and evil could happen to us.

In these moments, we are scared together.

We text each other and call each other. We send out DMs with only two words: *You ok?* There is a collective experience we are sharing when the humanity of even one of us has been violated. This is the community hurt we shoulder. It is also the community hope we sink into. Because when we are scared, we also grieve together. We hold vigils together. We light candles together. We remember together.

We also organize together. We protest together. We march together. We propose solutions together. We join our voices together, and this becomes our hope. We hope that change is still possible. We push back against the evil and determine that we will not let this violation hide in the musty annals of history, collecting dust. We face the fear. We face the abominable. And we live.

The day after the shooting, I could feel my fear and anger turn into defiance. I got out of bed. I got dressed. And I drove to my church. I cried the whole way. I sat in one of the pews, with my back to the door, but only for a few moments. I was consumed by fear. I moved to the stairs just inside the doors of the church, which were swung open, letting in the noise from passing cars. I didn't have to sit there alone. A handful of members sat on those stairs with me. We cried and sang and prayed. We were all still struggling against our fear. But we were also reaffirming our human right to safety. We were reclaiming our space. We were experiencing both community hurt and community hope.

Being a racial justice educator didn't save me from being afraid or angry or devastated. By this time I had already been deeply impacted by the deaths of Trayvon Martin, Michael Brown, my own cousin Dalin, and many others. Sadly, this mass shooting at Mother Emanuel wouldn't be the end of my pain or fear or devastation. I felt it again with Sandra Bland and Breonna Taylor and George Floyd, and the list is just becoming too long to bear.

But every time, I also experience again the love of the

Black community. I survive on our intimacy—online, in real life, in the Church and outside of it. I become baptized again into the tradition of Black love—love for self and love for one another. And because of that love, I can continue on.

BOUNDARIES

▬▬▬▬

Years ago I decided to teach classes on racial justice at the multiracial church where I worked. They were free for anyone to attend. I created three different classes where participants would progressively build on their knowledge. All they had to do was attend three weeks in a row. The class was a hit, so I kept teaching those sessions and added more. It was a lot of fun to discover how many people at the church were interested in racial justice and wanted to learn more.

But. (You knew there was a *but* coming, right?)

There was a guy who came to the first class, and I didn't see him again—until he bumped into me in the church lobby weeks later. He made a beeline straight for me and said, "Austin, I attended your first class, but I didn't come back after that, but I've been thinking and I have some questions."

I blinked once. I blinked again. And I said, "No. No, I don't think you have any questions *for me.* Because if you had questions *for me,* you would have come back to class." And, of course, I invited him to come back when the class started over again.

Why did I respond like that? Because I was setting a boundary—my brain was available once a week for free through these classes. And now he wanted it to be free after church service when all I was thinking about was where I wanted to eat? Nope. Meet this good boundary.

I wasn't always good at putting boundaries in place around my work. In fact, I wasn't even sure I was allowed to put boundaries in place. Wasn't I supposed to take every opportunity to teach someone else? Wasn't I supposed to correct any and all racist inaccuracies? Was I personally disappointing Rosa Parks and the entire Black community if I didn't push back every chance I got?

This expectation had been set for me long before I was being paid to host classes and workshops. Teachers assigned books by white authors every year, then expected me to speak on the Black Experience when one Black character made an appearance in the story. Classmates expected me to engage in debates about affirmative action or reparations as they "played devil's advocate" (as if the devil needed any advocates). Sometimes people expected me to be knowledgeable about hip-hop or the hood or other random topics they assumed I would know. For years, I was basically the substitute teacher when it came to talking about being Black in America. That's why classrooms like Mr. Slivinski's and Professor McMath's and Dr. Simms's were so unusual. In so many white spaces, the assumption that I could speak on behalf of all Black people was the norm.

Nothing of note happened to make me start questioning this expectation. The truth is I just got tired and then annoyed. It felt like everywhere I went, people were treating me like a vending machine. Insert some coins and Austin will effortlessly spit out some knowledge. Few people seemed to respect that I had worked hard for this knowledge and that it was real work to teach about racial justice (or injustice) in America.

I started imagining that I was filling a jar with all my wisdom if every piece of wisdom I earned was represented by one dollar. Every history book I'd read received a dollar. Every article I read received one dollar. Every conversation I'd had about what it's like to be Black received a dollar. Everything I'd learned from my parents, my grandparents, my cousins, my friends—added more dollars. Forget a jar, I was already looking at stacks, but I kept going. Every minute I spent pondering what it means to be Black or writing about Blackness was one more dollar. I mentally tallied every piece of art in my home, scrolled through my playlists, assessed the authors on my shelves, still adding imaginary dollars. I counted every drama, every documentary, every video I watched to learn more about race in America. When my little thought exercise was over, I realized I had a whole bank's worth of information, knowledge, and stories. Everything I knew about being Black had required my thoughtfulness, engagement, energy, and time. It required taking out student loans, furthering my education, and writing like my life depended on it. My bank would be enormous. I bet yours would be, too.

I started asking myself: When a random white person has an opinion about race, does that mean I am required to open the doors of my bank and respond?

Nope.

I've worked hard to collect this valuable information—and it is valuable. So I have the right to decide my bank's open and closed hours. I am usually willing to open the doors for my closest friends, because they will treat the effort with respect and sincerity. I am often willing to open the bank for unique opportunities to inspire change—like when challenging the leadership of an organization or hosting a teach-in that I am passionate about. I enjoy opening the doors for a program, lecture, or workshop that I created. I love when I get to collaborate with other agents of change. The result can be magical.

I have often been treated like a vending machine, but rejecting that framing was an important turning point for me. I am not Coca-Cola out here. I am a whole human being, and I get to prioritize how, when, and where I impart knowledge about racial justice. Because sometimes I have other things to do—like watch *Black Panther,* dance in the mirror to Beyoncé's *Homecoming,* or hang with my friends. And, honestly, I don't think Rosa Parks is disappointed by any of those choices.

NO MORE SHRINKING

I wouldn't trade being a Black girl for anything in the world. And, for all the reasons we've talked about in this book, being a Black girl isn't always easy. You're not just dealing with breakups and friend fallouts, and the academic pressures that all students have to navigate. In many cases, you will also have to deal with racism. And sometimes that racism is the expectation that you will shrink. As you start to grow confident in who you are, it's possible that others will resent that confidence. They will expect you to mirror their low expectations. And when you refuse to comply—when you set your own standard—they will do everything they can to bring you down to where they are.

In college I was a resident adviser, which basically means I was in charge of making sure all the people on my floor stayed safe. I had to walk around and check on people. I received calls from worried parents. If a student was sick or needed to go to the hospital, I often was the one helping to coordinate transportation.

But I had another job as resident adviser, too. Whenever I was working behind the desk in the lobby of our building, I was responsible for checking the ID of anyone who came in. That way we always knew who was in the building at any given time.

One day I was sitting behind the front lobby desk, and a white kid who wasn't a student came to visit a resident. I told him I needed his ID before he could go up to the person's room. He refused, but I stood firm. I told him he could call the person down and hang in the lobby, but he wasn't going upstairs without leaving his ID with me.

We were in a standoff. He didn't want to hand over his ID, and I wouldn't let him go. Then he hurled the N-word at me.

I must tell you that this white guy was dressed in an oversize white T-shirt and superbaggy jeans, with three or four gold chains around his neck. Yet he wasn't coming close to embodying the Black cool he was trying on like a sad costume. So when he called me the N-word, all I could do was laugh in his face at the foolishness.

He was clearly mad that I was a Black girl who was in charge. But that was his problem, not mine. And I cannot close out this book without reminding you that when other people are offended by your confidence, your power, your existence, that's their problem, not yours.

You are not responsible for making other people feel more comfortable that you are the valedictorian of your school or that your coach made you the captain of the team or that your presentation is the one that will go down in infamy. You do not need to apologize for winning the spelling bee or speech contest or coding competition. You do not need to make yourself smaller for the sake of small-minded people who don't see you for who you are. No shrinking.

Head high.

You may be told that you need to be more modest about your skills, talents, or accomplishments. But Dr. Maya Angelou, the great poet and author, taught us that "modesty is a learned affectation." This is a beautiful way of saying that many women (especially Black women) learn to make ourselves smaller, to downplay our accomplishments, to speak softly, because it's expected of us. We learn how to wear modesty like a frilly dress that no one will be intimidated by.

Instead of being modest, Dr. Angelou encourages us to practice humility. She said, "Humility comes from the inside out. It says someone was here before me and

I'm here because I've been paid for. I have something to do and I will do that because I'm paying for someone else who has yet to come."

There is no need to be shy about your accomplishments. You are able to achieve because other Black women paved the way for you. And now you will join them in paving the way for others. That is not something to be shy or modest about. Confidence and humility. That's what we want to cultivate in our lives and in the lives of the Black girls around us. Let's hold our heads high while we celebrate our sisters and ourselves.

JOY

———

Fighting for the lives of Black people is an important part of my work, and I was all-in long before I got paid to do it. As a college student, I was always stirring up trouble or calling people out or creating safe spaces for other students like me. And I enjoyed it. It wasn't a burden to fight for myself. Now I'm a professional fighter. I am paid to write books, lecture, offer workshops, and present opportunities to learn about antiracism. I love my work. I love being involved in the fight. But the fight was—and is—still only one part of who I am. It's also only one part of who you are.

As a Black kid, you have a right to your anger over the injustice you face. But you also have a right to joy. I want profound joy for you.

There will always be something to fight for, but you are worth fighting for, too. You must learn how to enjoy

joy, how to protect your peace, how to remember that you are fully human: capable of fighting but entitled to resting.

I want you to fall in love and go to parties. I want you to travel the world and dance in front of your bedroom mirror. I want you to roller-skate and check out the latest movies. I want you to volunteer or try an internship or get a job at the mall. I want you to draw and write stories and try out for the school play. I want you to play sports and enjoy practice and celebrate wins with pizza and ice cream. I want you to have your own epic coming-of-age story. I want you to develop your own style. I want you to discover which cut of underwear you like best and how high or short you prefer your socks. I want you to enjoy nature. I want you to blow dandelion seeds, count clover leaves, and chase fireflies. I want you to climb trees and ride your bike and go swimming. I want you to enjoy your life right now. I want you to fall in love with the sound of your own laughter.

I want your life to be about more than The Struggle. I want you to live—really live.

The more you learn about injustice in the world, the harder this will be. You might even start to feel guilty when good things happen because you are so aware of all the bad things in the world.

It's messy. It messes with your heart.

But the absence of your joy isn't going to fix the world. We can't treat these broken systems like trading cards, where you give up some joy and in return get some justice. It doesn't work like that.

So many of us are on the journey of figuring out what it looks like to pursue both justice and joy. If I can't trade one for the other, how can they both live together, side by side, in my body, in my work, in my life?

You know, I recently tried to make a list of the things that bring me joy. Can I confess that it was a pretty short list? It went as follows:

Things ACB Loves

- Reading mysteries
- Witnessing the process of artists
- Ice cream
- Face masks
- Breakfast

That's it. That was my list. That was my first attempt to think about the things that bring me joy. And I quickly realized that I spent so much time stuffing myself with more knowledge about injustice, it kept me from becoming knowledgeable about my own joy.

It's wild to really think about how even good work,

like the pursuit of racial justice, can swallow you whole, can make you feel like your joy is secondary to the work instead of a vital part of the work and of your life.

So I kept working on my list. It now includes:

- Movies
- Naps
- Antiques
- Interior design
- Magazines
- The sound of birds chirping
- The feel of the sun
- The sound of the ocean

My list may still be a little short, but I'm adding to it every day. I'm exploring leisure. I'm remembering the things I used to love, and I'm trying them again. I recently bought a bicycle. I hadn't been on a bicycle in years, but I loved riding as a kid. Now that I'm no longer falling off my new bike, I'm contemplating buying a basket so I can put flowers and other dainty objects in it while I frolic. Frolicking is going on the list.

Never lose sight of the things that bring you joy. I want your list to be as long as the earth is from the sun. I want you to know that joy is yours.

The hard things will come. I cannot save you from

experiencing America's devasting history and present. I cannot save you from knowing community hurt or asking your own questions rooted in fear. I cannot prevent new terrors or save you from the ones you've already experienced. But I will offer you this invitation into Black love. I will encourage you to indulge in community hope. We can experience more than fear. We can be defiant. We can be brave. We can find safety in one another. Please do not experience community hurt and then deny yourself community hope. Both are important. The joy will sustain you when the pain feels unbearable. You are worthy of hope and joy.

So crack jokes with one another.

Go to amusement parks, enjoy road trips, and create your own adventure.

Gather together—whether at church or a poetry class or a sports team or a dance troupe or a robotics club.

Sit with your friends at the lunch table or with your cousins around the dinner table or with your parents and siblings around the coffee table.

Head to the beauty salon or barbershop or community meeting or family reunion.

Let there be no shame, only joy, in needing connection, in needing Black love. It just might save your life, like it has saved mine—a million times over.

ACKNOWLEDGMENTS

This book would not exist without a whole host of people who believed in this project before I had written a single word. To my agent, Margaret Riley King; my editor, Derek Reed; and my collaborator, Andrea Williams: Thank you for your patient hand-holding and deep belief that I could do this. Your suggestions, feedback, and editorial eye made all the difference.

Thanks also to my friends who had to listen to me try out a million ideas and ask a million questions throughout this process. Amena Brown, JoAnn Saxton, Glennon Doyle, Lisa Cockrel, and Bunmi Ishola—thank you for believing when I was ready to throw in the towel. Thank you for your encouragement and deep belief that I could do this. To my early readers Andrea Price, Zakiya Jackson, and Karla Mendoza, y'all came through for your girl, and I'm so grateful that you did. Thanks also to my team: Stephanie McBee, Brooke Campbell, and Jenny Booth Potter, for being sensitive to the roller coaster of writing a book and for always making space for me.

I never would have become a writer if not for the sacrifices of my parents, the impact of my mentors, and the support of my husband. Tommie Brown, I could not ask for a better partner in love, in friendship, or in my career. I'm so blessed to be loved by you.

And to my little boy, you are absolute magic. You bring me joy.

ABOUT THE AUTHOR

Austin Channing Brown is a speaker, writer, and media producer providing inspired leadership on racial justice in America. She is the *New York Times* bestselling author of *I'm Still Here: Black Dignity in a World Made for Whiteness,* a Reese's Book Club pick; and the CEO of Herself Media. She lives in metro-Detroit with her husband, son, and puppy.

ABOUT THE TYPE

This book was set in Garamond, a typeface originally designed by the Parisian type cutter Claude Garamond (c. 1500–61). This version of Garamond was modeled on a 1592 specimen sheet from the Egenolff-Berner foundry, which was produced from types assumed to have been brought to Frankfurt by the punch cutter Jacques Sabon (c. 1520–80). Claude Garamond's distinguished romans and italics first appeared in *Opera Ciceronis* in 1543–44. The Garamond types are clear, open, and elegant.